COMPACT
CYMRU

CW00448137

The Rocks of Wales:
their story

Dyfed Elis-Gruffydd

Gwasg Carreg Gwalch

First published in 2019
© text: Dyfed Elis-Gruffydd

ISBN: 978-1-84524-295-4
Cover design: Eleri Owen

Published by Gwasg Carreg Gwalch,
12 Iard yr Orsaf, Llanrwst, Wales LL26 0EH
tel: 01492 642031
email: books@carreg-gwalch.cymru
website: www.carreg-gwalch.cymru

1. Rock climbing in the Llŷn peninsula;
2. The Green Bridge of Wales © Gwasg Carreg Gwalch

Contents

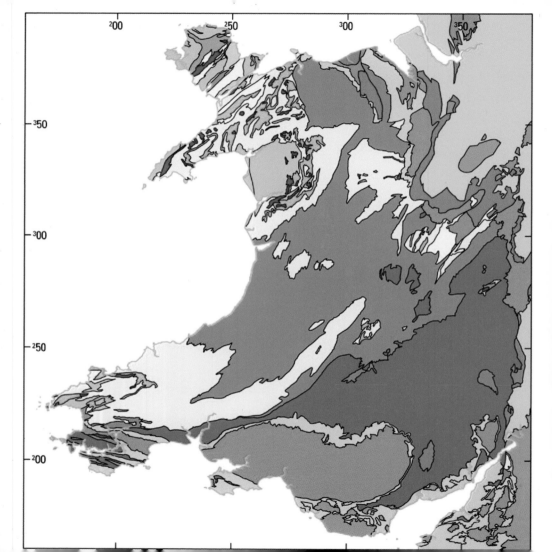

The Rocks of Wales: their story

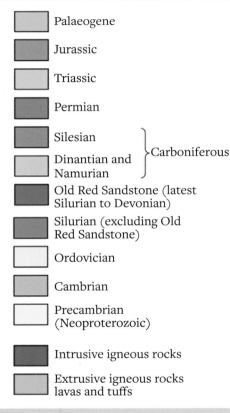

Palaeogene

Jurassic

Triassic

Permian

Silesian

Dinantian and Namurian

} Carboniferous

Old Red Sandstone (latest Silurian to Devonian)

Silurian (excluding Old Red Sandstone)

Ordovician

Cambrian

Precambrian (Neoproterozoic)

Intrusive igneous rocks

Extrusive igneous rocks lavas and tuffs

Geological map of Wales © *British Geological Survey*

Introduction

Although small in area, Wales has one of the most diverse range of rocks to be found anywhere in the world. As a consequence, the geological map of the country, recording the distribution of rocks of different ages and types, is a wondrous and unrivalled kaleidoscope of colour, a veritable work of art. Unsurprisingly, given its exceedingly rich geological heritage, Wales is also recognized as one of the birthplaces of the science of geology. Furthermore, the country's spectacular landscapes, including its breathtaking coastline, which annually attract a multitude of climbers, walkers and less venturesome tourists, are largely a reflection of the character of the underlying, age-old rocks which have, over the millennia, been squeezed, ripped apart, fractured and suffered the erosive onslaught of rivers, glaciers and waves.

Though undeniably old, the rocks from which the Welsh landform has been fashioned were once thought to be of

Bust of Edward Llwyd (Lhuyd) outside the Centre for Advanced Welsh and Celtic Studies, Aberystwyth

relatively recent origin. As those few present-day readers of the King James Bible, published in 1701, know full well, the enigmatic inscription 'Before Christ 4004' or '4004 BC' printed either in the margins or between two columns of the opening verses of the Book of Genesis was the date of the Creation arrived at by James Ussher (1581–1656), Archbishop of Armagh, in Ireland. Ussher was a man of considerable scholarship and his assertion that Creation took place during the evening of Saturday, 22 October 4004 BC was actually based on many years of study of biblical texts and other sources. Nevertheless, his claim that the Earth, including its oldest rocks, was some 6,000 years old did not go unchallenged.

In a letter penned by Welshman Edward Llwyd (Lhuyd; *c.*1660–1709) in 1691, during the year that he was appointed keeper of the Ashmolean Museum, Oxford, Llwyd the accomplished naturalist drew attention to the thousands of 'vast stones' encountered on the floor of both Nant Peris and Nant Ffrancon, two of Snowdonia's most well-known valleys. Although the boulders are now known to have been deposited during the retreat of

Nant Ffrancon © *Gwasg Carreg Gwalch*

'ice age' glaciers some 15,000 years ago, Llwyd erroneously maintained that since 'there are but two or three that have fallen [downslope under the influence of gravity] in the memory of any man now living . . . we shall be compelled to allow the rest many thousands of years more than the age of the world'. Since most adults at the time lived until their sixties, over a period of 60 years two or three boulders were deemed likely to have fallen, one every 20 to 30 years. Assuming that a mere 10,000 boulders lie on the floor of Llanberis, the Earth including its oldest rocks, according to Llwydian logic, was at least 200,000 years old, very much older than Ussher's estimate.

Time immemorial

During the 300 and more years that have elapsed since Llwyd's untimely death, Earth's age has been set further and further back in time, especially during the twentieth century. Following the discovery of radioactivity and that radioactive elements in rocks decay at constant rates, it became possible to date the chapters of Earth's mind-blowingly long history. Geologists nowadays are accustomed to talking in blasé fashion about rocks millions or billions of years old. However, in order to make the enormity of geological time – that part of the Earth's history that is recorded in the rocks of Wales – somewhat more comprehensible to non-geologists, it's helpful to place some of Wales' key geological events in everday units of time by compressing the entire 4.4 billion years that have elapsed since the formation of the oldest known rock fragment in the world into a single year.

On that scale and on the assumption that the Earth's oldest rocks were formed on the first of January, ten months elapsed prior to the formation of the oldest rocks on mainland Wales, that are to be found stradling the Welsh-English border near Kington (Ceintun). Anglesey could lay claim to similar ancient rocks that had come into being a week later than those on the mainland. On the 24th of November violent volcanic eruptions not only led to the formation of many of Snowdonia's rocks but also those of Pembrokeshire. Land plants made their first appearance on the 28th of November, about four days after the cessation of volcanic activity. Thick layers of limestone, now encountered in north-east Wales, Anglesey and the length and breadth of south Wales, were being deposited on the floor of warm, tropical seas on the third of December and three days later, the growth of widespread tropical swamps led to the formation of the coalfields of south and north-east Wales. Mid December witnessed the death of a dinosaur whose fossil was discovered within the youngest rocks of Wales, layer upon layers of limestone and mudstone that are the foundation of the magnificent coastal cliffs of the Vale of Glamorgan.

If the enormity of geological time is difficult to comprehend, the ability of geologists to speak in terms of both hard and soft rocks is a concept not readily understood by those with little or no prior knowledge of geology. Technically speaking, any aggregate of minerals or organic matter, whether consolidated or not, is a rock. So the definition of a rock includes 'soft', unconsolidated materials such as sands, gravels and clays, although in ordinary usage such earth materials are more commonly referred to as superficial deposits, that have generally accumulated through the action of wind, water or ice during very recent geological times.

What follows is neither a blow-by-blow account of the rocks of Wales nor a scholarly earth-science textbook, but rather a geological odyssey that seeks to raise the awareness of inquisitive members of the general reading public as to the origin and significance of the rocks and minerals beneath their feet and the remarkable and exciting story that they record. It's a journey through time, whose story is told chapter-by-chronological chapter by focussing attention in turn on ten particular areas of Wales where the rocks of a known age are well-displayed. In so doing, every attempt has been made to avoid as many technical terms as possible. Those that are included are explained in the Glossary.

1. Anglesey and the Llŷn peninsula

Precambrian [c.700–543 million years ago] – Cambrian [543–490 million years ago]

Contains Ordnance Survey data
© Crown copyright and database right 2018

It's been suggested, rather unkindly, that Anglesey's rolling plateau surface, some 75 metres above sea level, is no more that a convenient platform from which to view the grandeur of Snowdonia (Eryri). This notion was delivered a crushing blow in 2005, however, when the island became a member of the European Geoparks Network and the UNESCO Global Network in recognition, at least in part, of its rich geological heritage and the worldwide importance of Anglesey's geology.

But what about Llŷn, that 'branch of rock suspended between the sea and heaven' (*cangen o graig ynghrog rhwng y môr a'r nefoedd*)? In the opinion of the celebrated English-language poet and Welsh-language author and naturalist R.S. Thomas (1913–2000), who penned that

1. *Mynydd Bodafon*; 2. *Andrew Crombie Ramsay*

memorable description, the peninsula is only a platform from which to appreciate the rest of Wales! That said, R.S. was acutely aware of the 'awesome and incredible age of Aberdaron's rocks' (*oed ofnadwy ac anhygoel creigiau Aberdaron*) and that it's simply not possible to 'live on the Llŷn peninsula without being mindful of the Earth's great age' (*ni fedrwch fyw yn Llŷn heb gofio am oed mawr y Ddaear*).

The first person to hint at the great age of some of Anglesey's rocks was Andrew Crombie Ramsay, a member of the Geological Survey of Great Britain who was destined to become its director-general in 1871. In 1849, the young geologist had arranged to visit the island in the company of the Survey's first director, Sir Henry De la Beche. 'I met Sir H. on Saturday at Bangor', he recalls: 'We had a short rap at Anglesey at very old rocks – older than the Cambrian.' But it was not only the presence of ancient rocks that drew Andrew Ramsay to the island. In the summer of 1850, he had spent a few days at the home of the Reverend James Williams, the Rector of Llanfair-yng-Nghornwy, and the great-grandfather of one of Wales' most famous contemporary artists, Sir Kyffin Williams (1918–2006). It was there in the Rectory that Ramsay fell in love with Louisa, one of James and Frances Williams' four children, whom he married on 20 July 1852.

Fourteen years later, Ramsay's *magnum opus*, *The Geology of North Wales* (1866), was published, a second edition of which appeared in 1881. But as author of what was then considered to be 'the most important work which has been issued by the Geological Survey', he was required to toe the party line and not rock the geological boat by maintaining the presence on the island of rocks 'older than the Cambrian'. In keeping with the Survey's steadfast refusal at the time to recognize the existence of rocks of Precambrian age – despite the fact that such a notion had been advocated by vociferous 'amateurs' such as Dr Henry Hicks in Pembrokeshire – Ramsay, now a senior member of the geological

MEMOIRS OF THE GEOLOGICAL SURVEY

OF

GREAT BRITAIN

AND OF THE

MUSEUM OF PRACTICAL GEOLOGY.

THE GEOLOGY OF NORTH WALES,

BY

A. C. RAMSAY, LL.D., F.R.S.,

DIRECTOR-GENERAL OF THE GEOLOGICAL SURVEY OF THE UNITED KINGDOM AND MUSEUM OF PRACTICAL GEOLOGY.

WITH AN APPENDIX ON THE FOSSILS,

BY

J. W. SALTER, A.L.S., F.G.S.

REVISED AND ADDED TO BY ROBERT ETHERIDGE, F.R.S.,

PALÆONTOLOGIST TO THE SURVEY.

SECOND EDITION.

PUBLISHED BY ORDER OF THE LORDS COMMISSIONERS OF HER MAJESTY'S TREASURY.

LONDON:

PRINTED FOR HER MAJESTY'S STATIONERY OFFICE,

AND SOLD BY

LONGMAN & Co., Paternoster Row ; TRÜBNER & Co., Ludgate Hill ;
LETTS & SON, 33, King William Street ; EDWARD STANFORD, 6, Charing Cross ;
and J. WYLD, 12, Charing Cross :

ALSO BY

Messrs. JOHNSTON, 4, St. Andrew Square, Edinburgh :
HODGES, FOSTER, & Cc., 104, Grafton Street, and A. THOM, Abbey Street, Dublin.

1881.

Price One Guinea.

1. *Ramsay's gravestone, Llansadwrn Church. The boulder of Carboniferous limestone is a glacial erratic transported south-westwards from nearby Penmon;* 2. *Coedana granite: detail of a boulder that resides in the National Botanic Garden of Wales; 3. Edward Greenly's grave, Llangristiolus. Surprisingly, the red granite gravestones are not native to Anglesey*

IN SACRED
MEMORY OF
Ed. GREENLY
DSc. F. G. S.
1861 — 1951

ALSO HIS
DEVOTED WIFE
ANNIE
1852 — 1927
REUNITED

'establishment', had changed his tune: 'The oldest rocks in Wales . . . rise to the surface in . . . Anglesey, the greater portion of which consist of . . . schists, gneissic rocks, grits and quartz-rock, all considered to be of Cambrian age.' Also listed amongst the 'oldest rocks of Wales' were the 'ancient schists' of Llŷn, that form a broad belt of land between Porth Dinllaen and Bardsey Island (Ynys Enlli). But a much more cautious note was sounded by Ramsay – whose remains lie buried in the cemetery surrounding the attractive little church of Llansadwrn – regarding these latter rocks. They, too, he speculated, are 'supposed to be of Cambrian age'!

Separated from the mainland by the tide-ripped Menai Strait (Afon Menai) – deepened by torrents of glacial meltwater flowing along the belt of broken bedrock that marks the line of the Menai Strait Fault (and later drowned as sea level rose after the last 'ice age') – the history of Anglesey's ancient rocks is nothing if not complicated and contentious. After cutting his geological teeth mapping a part of the Highlands of Scotland, Edward Greenly turned his attention to Anglesey. But so numerous and so varied were the problems encountered, that the task of preparing his exhaustive 980 page, two-volume memoir on the island's geology (*The Geology of Anglesey*) published in 1919, together with an exquisite one inch to one mile geological map that appeared in 1920, had occupied his energies for 24 years! Unlike Ramsay, Greenly – who is buried in the cemetery of St Cristiolus' Church overlooking Malltraeth Marsh (Cors Ddyga) – was in no doubt that the island's oldest rocks were all of Precambrian age. But, not surprisingly, given the plethora of rock-types (he himself had identified about 70 different types), the highly complex pattern of folds and faults (described by him as being 'involved in the extreme'), and the fact that most of the ancient rocks, which occupy about two-thirds of the island's interior, remain hidden under a blanket of glacial deposits, not all of Greenly's conclusions have stood the test of time.

On the eastern outskirts of Gwalchmai lies the permanent site of Primin Môn, Anglesey's annual and highly-acclaimed agricultural show. But that's not the village's only claim to fame, for in a quarry less than a kilometre west of the village Coedana granite is exposed, the island's oldest radiometrically-dated Precambrian igneous rock. The granite, traceable in a band north-east and south-west of Gwalchmai, was formed from molten rock (magma) that slowly cooled and crystallized in a vast subterranean chamber about 614 million years ago. But because the magma forced its way into the midst of pre-existing rocks, the Coedana granite cannot lay claim to being the oldest of Anglesey's Precambrian rocks. That particular distinction belongs to a suite of intensely altered metamorphic rocks (gneiss), unbelievably ancient crustal rocks into which the granite was intruded. Indeed, the granite is thought to have been derived from the melting of the crustal rocks over 1,300 million years ago!

To encounter other rocks of undoubted Precambrian age – those whose age exceeds 542 million years – you will need to head south-east from Gwalchmai to Llanfair Pwllgwyngyll (abbreviated to Llanfair-pwll or Llanfair PG), along the Holyhead (Caergybi) road, the A5(T), completed by the celebrated engineer Thomas Telford early in the nineteenth century. Besides the well-known addition to the village's name – Llanfair Pwllgwyngyll-*gogerychwyrndrobwll-*

The Anglesey Column

llantysiliogogogoch (which is no more than a fanciful appendage coined in 1869 by a local tailor to tickle the fancy of gullible and bemused visitors arriving at the railway station that was in danger of becoming redundant following completion in 1850 of Robert Stephenson's Britannia Bridge [Pont Britannia]) – a notable landmark at journey's end is the Anglesey Column (Tŵr Marcwis). Built in 1816-17 of Carboniferous limestone quarried at Moelfre, the 34-metre-high Greek Doric column supports a 4-metre-high bronze statue of Henry William Paget, 1st Marquis of Anglesey, of Waterloo fame, placed atop his perch in 1860.

From the platform at the top of the tower (closed since 2012 in order to execute essential repairs) visitors were confronted by a wonderful all-round panorama of Anglesey, the Menai Strait and the towering summits of Snowdonia. But geologically, the site is of great interest because it includes the best and most accessible outcrops in Britain of a very unusual rock, called blue-schist on account of the presence of the blue-coloured mineral glaucophane. These 560–550 million-year-old Precambrian rocks, upon which the Anglesey Column stands, have had a torrid history for they are only found where the Earth's rigid, tectonic plates converge and collide and one oceanic plate, composed mainly of basalt lava, is forced down (subducted)

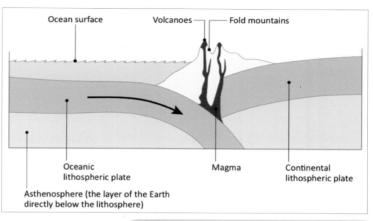

Cross-section through two colliding tectonic plates

below a continental plate and ultimately altered (metamorphosed) under an unusual combination of high pressures and relatively low temperatures. As a consequence, blue-schists are only rarely encountered and those exposed near Llanfair-pwll are famous for they are amongst the oldest such rocks in the world.

But to gain an unforgettable impression of how rocks forming the Earth's crust can be deformed as a consequence of colliding crustal plates, the tiny lighthouse-capped island of South Stack (Ynys Lawd) is the place to be. Because of the fantastic large and small-scale folds visible in the magnificent sea cliffs of South Stack and neighbouring Holy Island (Ynys Gybi) – linked to mainland Anglesey's western seaboard by way of a causeway – it ranks as one of the sites most visited by geologists. Described by Greenly as an 'amazing revelation', the alternate layers of sandstones and silty mudstones, metamorphosed and spectacularly crumpled by enormous pressures within the Earth's crust, still retain evidence of having originally accumulated in the form of a huge deep-sea fan, fed by turbulent and dense clouds of sand, silt and mud-laden currents that were repeatedly swept off an ancient, shallow continental shelf.

The spectacularly folded strata of the so-called South Stack Formation are overlain by the Holyhead Quarzite Formation, a pile of sandstones, mudstones and quartzite that underpin nearby Holyhead Mountain (Mynydd Twr). They too are the product of powerful turbidity currents. The 220-metre-high rocky summit of Mynydd Twr – topped by the Iron Age fort of Caer y Twr

which provided its hardy inhabitants with one of the great vistas of Wales – owes its height and prominence to the hard, white quartzites that have stubbornly resisted the agents of weathering and erosion alike. Not surprisingly, given its toughness, extensive use was made of the quartzite, which was extracted from now defunct quarries at the north-eastern end of the mountain, for the construction of the enormous Holyhead Harbour breakwater, an impressive structure finally completed in 1873. Some years later, the purest quartzite extracted from the same quarries was used on-site in the manufacture of heat-resistant silica bricks. The old brickworks chimney still stands and is an imposing feature of the Holyhead Breakwater Country Park.

If the rocks of South Stack provide one of the most iconic and memorable geological localities in Britain, the coastline in the vicinity of Rhoscolyn, at the southern end of Holy Island, has been described as 'the best place in Great Britain' to see and study 'the effects of

1. White quartzite, Holyhead Mountain;
2. Bwa Gwyn, a natural arch comprised of white quartz; © Paul Gasson@gmail.com
3. South Stack © Gwasg Carreg Gwalch

folding and cleavage formation on a sequence of bedded sedimentary rocks' (cleavage is the closely-spaced, parallel planes of weakness along which rocks such as slate and schist tend to split). Head for the coast south-west of Rhoscolyn, and pause for a while at the old Coastguard Station that stands alongside the Isle of Anglesey Coastal Path. Hereabouts you're standing on the crest of a major up-fold, the Rhoscolyn Anticline. By walking a short distance south-east along the path, the intensely crumpled rocks – including, in places, highly contorted veins of white quartz – forming the south-eastern side of the anticline are superbly exposed in the coastal cliffs. Here, the geometry of many of the bewilderingly complex folds, the product of unimaginable tectonic forces, have been sculpted into striking three-dimensional forms by weathering. Head north along the Coastal Path and you will encounter Bwa Gwyn, a dazzling white (in sunshine!) natural arch that's considered to be one of the most spectacular features of coastal erosion at Rhoscolyn. Age-wise, the well-bedded

South Stack: folded layers of metamorphosed sandstones and mudstones

metamorphosed sandstones and mudstones of the Rhoscolyn Formation are the youngest strata of the South Stack Group (South Stack Formation, Holyhead Quarzite Formation and Rhoscolyn Formation) and like the sandstones and mudstones of South Stack and Holyhead Mountain they too represent layers of

Rocks of Wales

sand, silt and mud deposited in the form of a deep-sea fan by turbidity currents.

For many a long year, the metamorphosed sedimentary rocks of the South Stack Group were considered to be of Precambrian age, but not any more. Their secret has been unlocked, thanks to tiny grains of the mineral zircon. Because they contain uranium atoms that decay into lead at a known rate, zircons can be dated and it's now known that those derived from rocks belonging to the South Stack Formation are 522 million years old, 20 million years younger than the very youngest Precambrian rocks. Not only does this mean that the South Stack Group of rocks must be of Cambrian age, but that the overlying rocks of the New Harbour Group and Gwna Group, formerly considered to be Precambrian in age, must also have accumulated in Cambrian times!

In stark contrast to the stratified rocks of the South Stack Group, those of the New Harbour Group, that outcrop across much of Holy Island and north of a line joining Valley (Y Fali) and Amlwch, consist mainly of metamorphic rocks, silvery-green schists that were once a sequence of thinly-bedded layers of mud and silt. However, also recorded amongst the schists, characterized by tight, small-scale folds of bewildering complexity, are thin beds of jasper, basalt lava in the form of untidy piles of pillows and bodies of serpentinite, itself a metamorphic rock formed from the alteration of a coarse-grained, dark-coloured igneous rock. So attractive is the green and dark red serpentinite that it was quarried near Llanfechell and Rhoscolyn and marketed as 'Mona Marble' during the nineteenth century. Numerous adverts and articles extolling the virtues of the ornamental stone appeared in the press and examples of its decorative use can be found locally and further afield. For example, it was used in the construction of the W.O. Stanley monument in St Cybi's parish church in Holyhead (W.O. Stanley of Penrhos was Anglesey's Member of Parliament between 1837 and 1847) and it also appears in the form of chimney-pieces in the drawing-room of Penrhyn Castle, a gigantic neo-Norman nineteenth-century mansion house near Bangor, home of the Pennant family and once owners of the Penrhyn slate quarry near Bethesda.

Succeeding the rocks of the New Harbour Group are the very varied rocks of the Gwna Group, that outcrop not only

WILLIAM OWEN STANLEY OF PENRHOS

between Porth Dinllaen and Bardsey Island on the Llŷn peninsula, but also on mainland Anglesey, south-west of Llangefni and between Llanddona and Newborough (Niwbwrch). The Gwna Group is noted for its *mélange*, a French word meaning 'a mixture' adopted by Edward Greenly to describe, for the very first time in the world, a very peculiar deposit composed of a chaotic and jumbled mixture of rock-types of all shapes and sizes – from millimetres to kilometres across – set within a matrix of sand and mud. Within the cliffs of Trwyn Maen Melyn, south of Mynydd Mawr (160 m) at the westernmost tip of the Llŷn peninsula, walkers following the Wales Coast Path (Llwybr Arfordir Cymru) are confronted by gigantic boulders of white quartzite set in a mangled matrix of mudstone. As impressive in Anglesey, are the large masses of grey and brown limestone and white quartzite within the *mélange* exposed in the cliffs in the vicinity of Llanbadrig church (which according to

tradition was established by Saint Patrick before setting off for Ireland) and within sight of the Wylfa Nuclear Power Station, which ceased generating electricity in 2015. At the southernmost tip of Llanddwyn Island (Ynys Llanddwyn) the Gwna *mélange* is at its most colourful. Hereabouts are black volcanic rocks, red jasper, pink quartzite and multicoloured mudstones and sandstones. In all probability, the *mélange* is the product of colossal submarine landslides, for similar chaotic deposits are associated with giant earthquake-triggered slides, such as the Storegga slide off the coast of Norway, that covers about 112,500 square kilometers of the sea floor.

Though beloved by geologists, no visit to Anglesey is complete without a pilgrimage to Ynys Llanddwyn, for here in the sixth century, Dwynwen, the patron saint of lovers – whose holy-day is celebrated on the 25th of January – founded a church, now ruined, following her rejection of her over-enthusiastic suitor, Maelon. Whether she herself gained solace from the magnificent view south to the serrated outlines of Snowdonia, the blue silhouettes of Yr Eifl and the smaller hills of Llŷn – which form a striking

1. *Trwyn Maen Melyn:* mélange; 2. *Site of former Mona Marble quarry near Llanfechell;* 3. *Monument to W.O. Stanley of Penrhos, St Cybi's Church, Holyhead. The monument rests on a foundation of Mona Marble*

backdrop to the wide sweep of Caernarfon Bay – is not known. But it is a glorious panorama that never fails to impress those who are drawn to Llanddwyn merely to see 'some of the best examples of oceanic pillow lavas in Great Britain'. What were once bulbous lumps of molten red-hot lava extruded from an underwater volcanic vent, now appear as an incongruous pile of blue-black, misshapen pillows at the northern end of the tiny, rocky island. Between the pillows are striking accumulations of red jasper and the presence of microfossils within them would appear to confirm that the Gwna Group of rocks are also Cambrian and not Precambrian in age.

But one perplexing question remains: how to explain the juxtaposition of at least three distinct 'blocks' of ancient rocks bounded by great fractures cutting deep into the Earth's crust. The Coedana granite and its associated metamorphic gneisses share no features in common with the blue-schists, its nearest but much younger Precambrian neighbour, and both are entirely different in character to the great pile of Cambrian rocks of the South Stack, New Harbour and Gwna groups. And for good measure, all three disparate blocks are distinct from a narrow band of fault-bounded, Precambrian granitic and gabbroic intrusions, formed about 615 million years ago, abutting the Gwna *mélange* in Llŷn. It seems that these once-dispersed continental fragments, which can be likened to 'ships' of crustal material which 'sailed' across an ancient ocean, finally 'docked', or rather crashed into one another, amalgamating between about 700 and 530 million years ago to form part of the ancient microcontinent of Avalonia, that lay deep within the Cambrian southern hemisphere.

Leaving aside the subsequent northward drift of Avalonia, which was destined to collide with the larger continent of Baltica at the end of Ordovician and the beginning of Silurian times, no self-respecting geologist could turn his back on Anglesey before following the trail around Parys Mountain (Mynydd Parys), a magnificent, other-worldly, chromatic chasm that is Wales' most striking industrial landscape. Indeed, few would challenge the assertion of Jack and Susan Treagus, joint authors of *The Rocks of Anglesey's Coast* (2013), who maintain that Parys Mountain is 'one of the most dramatic landscapes anywhere in the

British Isles'. One hundred and fifty years of copper mining, which had its origins in Bronze age times, not only dis-embowelled the hill's summit but also covered it with huge piles of yellow, orange, red and brown debris which, acidified by the action of slowly oxidizing sulphide-ore minerals – such as copper pyrites, iron pyrites, galena (lead ore) and zinc blende – are reluctant to support a covering of vegetation. The metal ores are thought to have been deposited on the late Ordovician or early Silurian sea floor as hot mineral-rich solutions of volcanic origin, percolated up through the sea-bed rocks and sediments to form 'black smokers' – tall smoking 'chimneys'

1. Llanddwyn Island and Llŷn peninsula; © Gwasg Carreg Gwalch *2. Pillow lava, Llanddwyn Island*

composed entirely of sulphide-ore minerals. In its hey-day, during the second half of the eighteenth century, about 3.5 million tonnes of ore were mined, enough to produce 130,000 tonnes of copper. Production finally ceased in the mid nineteenth century but atop the nearby summit of Graig Wen the rather forlorn pit-head gear of Morris Shaft, sunk in 1988, is a reminder that mining companies have not abandoned all hope of reopening Mynydd Parys copper mine, once amongst the largest in the world.

1. Morris shaft; 2. Mynydd Parys (and opposite © Gwasg Carreg Gwalch)

2. The St David's peninsula (Pentir y Sant)

> Precambrian [c.700–543 million years ago]
> – Cambrian [543–490 million years ago]

Holyhead
ANGLESEY
Bangor
Bethesda
Caernarfon
1
LLŶN PENINSULA
SNOWDONIA
3
Harlech
Trawsfynydd
Dolgellau
Barmouth
CADAIR IDRIS
Bardsey Island
Prestatyn
Abergele
Holywell
St Asaph
Flint
Denbigh
Betws-y-coed
5
Rhuthun
Pentrefoelas
Wrexham
Llangollen
Aberdyfi
Y Borth
PUMLUMON
Aberystwyth
Llanidloes
Rhayader
New Quay
4
Cardigan
Cardigan Bay
2
St David's Head
PRESELY HILLS
St David's
St Bride's Bay
Skomer Island
Skokholm Island
St Ann's Head
8
Freshwater West
Manorbier
Tenby
Swansea
Neath
Pontypridd
BLACK MOUNTAIN
Brecon
BRECON BEACONS
BLACK MOUNTAINS
6
7
Aberdare
Merthyr Tudful
Blaenafon
Caerphilly
Bridgend
Ogmore-by-sea
9
Cardiff
Penarth
Barry Island

0 miles 20
0 kilometres 40
Contains Ordnance Survey data
© Crown copyright and database right 2018

The boggy floor of a sequestered valley may be an unprepossessing site on which to establish a great medieval church, but the seclusion of Glyn Rhosyn (the valley of the little bog) admirably served the needs of the reclusive monastic community established in the sixth century by Dewi (David), who in the early sixteenth century was recognized as the patron saint of Wales. Sadly, Dewi's monastery on the banks of the river Alun has disappeared without trace. So too has the cathedral established by Bernard, the first Norman bishop of St David's (Tyddewi), appointed by Henry I in 1115. But Bernard is remembered, for during his time Dewi was all but canonized by Pope Calixtus II, who decreed that two pilgrimages to St David's was equal to one to Rome. As a consequence, the present cathedral, begun under the direction of Bishop Peter de Leia in 1181 and transformed under the direction of Bishop Henry de Gower during the fourteenth century, became such an important destination for pilgrims during the Middle Ages, and remains so to this day.

A treasure of medieval architecture, the cathedral and the nearby fourteenth-century Bishop's Palace, built by Bishop

1. *St David's Cathedral sited on the floor of Glyn Rhosyn;.2 Glyn Rhosyn meltwater channel; 3. Cambrian conglomerate exposed on the Wales Coast Path overlooking St Non's Bay*

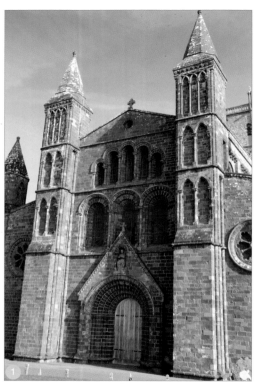

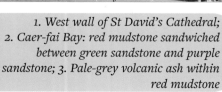

1. West wall of St David's Cathedral;
2. Caer-fai Bay: red mudstone sandwiched
between green sandstone and purple
sandstone; 3. Pale-grey volcanic ash within
red mudstone

Gower, are truly part of the landscape for both are constructed almost entirely of ancient rocks of Precambrian and Cambrian age, which form the rock-solid foundation of the St David's peninsula that juts boldly into the Irish Sea. But the sloping site and the unstable nature of the soft, saturated sediments on the floor of Glyn Rhosyn, a winding channel scoured by raging torrents of meltwater at the end of the last 'ice age', posed almost insurmountable problems for the cathedral builders. In 1220 the newly-erected tower collapsed, crushing the choir and transepts. Twenty-eight years later, the building was rocked and damaged by an earthquake, an event which probably caused the 'bulging condition of so great a part of the church'. Disconcerting for those visitors with an eye for details, the arcade pillars in the nave lean outwards and westwards, whilst the floor rises over four metres when traced from west to east! By the end of the eighteenth century, further urgent repairs were called for, because the west wall, which had already moved outwards by almost a metre, was threatening to bring down parts of the nave. But the rebuilding of the west wall by the famous architect John Nash (1752–1835) was to no avail. More substantial restoration work was desperately required. Alarmed by the perilous state of the tower, whose shift westwards had probably caused the outward movement of the west wall, George Gilbert Scott (1811–78) – designer, builder and renovator of numerous churches, cathedrals and workhouses – was called upon to undertake a major programme of restoration that began during the 1860s. Amazingly, he managed to avoid the task of rebuilding the tower from scratch by securing its foundations, but the west wall was dismantled and completely rebuilt – for the second time within the space of little more than half a century – with squared blocks of a dull-purple Cambrian sandstone acquired from quarries on the wave-battered cliffs of the peninsula's south coast.

In what was the first comprehensive survey of the coastline of England and Wales, published over seventy years ago, J.A. Steers maintained that 'It is, indeed, hard to think of coastal scenery in the British Isles more beautiful than the lichen- and plant-covered cliffs near St David's . . .' Almost without exception, the rocks magnificently exposed in the steep cliffs between Newgale (Niwgwl), at the head of the broad expanse of St Bride's Bay (Bae Sain Ffraid), and Porth Lisgi are sedimentary strata of Cambrian age, all deposited, layer by layer, in the waters of a sea slowly but surely encroaching upon an ancient and denuded Precambrian landmass that lay deep within the southern hemisphere. First to accumulate along those distant shores were masses of rounded pebbles and cobbles, followed by sand, mud, more sand and then mud again as the water deepened, all unconsolidated sediments subsequently transformed into layers of conglomerate, green sandstone, red mudstone, dull-purple and grey sandstones and dark grey-black mudstones. As a result of the convulsions of the Caledonian earth movements, that climaxed some 410 million years ago, the once near horizontal beds were unceremoniously upended so that they now plunge steeply seawards. So, to view the entire sequence of Lower to Middle Cambrian rocks, you need only visit a few sites along that section of the Wales Coast Path (Llwybr Arfordir Cymru) between Solfa (misspelt Solva) and Porth Clais.

Somewhere around the year 520, in a field above St Non's Bay (Bae Saint Non),

immediately south of St David's, Non gave birth to Dewi. The reputed site is marked by the ruins of a medieval chapel, dedicated to St Non, the foundations of which incorporate large squared blocks of conglomerate, a reddish rock that signals the birth of Cambrian times. Outcropping on the nearby Coast Path and forming a line of prominent sea stacks below the cliffs at the head of the bay, the conglomerate has the appearance of an ornamental concrete destined for garden rockeries, for it's packed with beach pebbles and cobbles of various kinds and colours, rounded by the incessant swash and backwash of ocean waves and later buried beneath thick layers of sand.

Sandwiched between thick layers of green sandstone and younger dull-purple sandstone, the thinner layers of bright red mudstones exposed in the cliffs that tower above the beautiful sandy beach of Caerfai Bay (Bae Caer-fai), east of St Non's Bay, are of special interest. Although not at all common, they do contain specimens of a fossil sea shell called *Lingulella*, the earliest Cambrian fossil found in south-west

1. Porth Clais: near vertical layers of Caerbwdi sandstone; 2. Caerbwdi Bay: site of Caerbwdi sandstone quarry; 3 Porth-y-rhaw

Wales. It's also a distant cousin of the 'living fossil' *Lingula* that's still with us today. But it's not only fossil shells that lurk within the red mudstones. There, too, for all to see are thin layers of pale-grey volcanic ash, known to have been hurled skywards about 519 million years ago by a succession of powerful and relatively local volcanic eruptions, before raining down on the sea surface and quietly sinking to the bottom. But that said, it's the dull-purple sandstone, overlying the red mudstones, which have grabbed the headlines.

Once quarried at both Caer-fai and neighbouring Caerbwdi, Caerbwdi sandstone was extensively used by medieval stonemasons to frame doors and windows of the cathedral and to face piers and arches inside the building. And during the late 1990s, planning permission was granted to reopen a small quarry at the head of Caerbwdi Bay in order to obtain sufficient material to replace badly weathered blocks in the cathedral's west wall and clerestory, and parts of the Bishop's Palace, which has been a ruin since the seventeenth century. Transportation of about 500 tonnes from Caerbwdi to the cathedral was a relatively simple matter but in medieval times, the distinctive sandstone was imported via Porth Clais, the harbour that served both the early monastic community and later medieval cathedral church at St David's. If we are to believe the legend recorded in the Mabinogion, it was also the landing-place of Twrch Trwyth, the fearsome wild boar chased by King Arthur and his knights over the Presely Hills and across the whole of south Wales. In much later times Porth Clais was an industrial harbour. But noxious fumes no longer emanate from the four nineteenth-century limekilns nor the gasworks, that up until 1950 stood on the site of the car park at the head of the inlet. The sheltered harbour now provides safe anchorage for pleasure craft, whilst the smooth, near vertical layers of Caerbwdi sandstone at its entrance are a favoured spot of climbers eager to hone their rock-climbing skills.

Whereas a search for fossils in the red mudstones of Caer-fai is enough to try the patience of a saint, fossil hunting amongst the beds of Caerbwdi sandstone is a futile occupation. None are to be found,

1. *Solfa: Trinity Quay; 2. Trwynhwrddyn: oucrop of the youngest Cambrian rocks; 3 Paradoxides davidis*

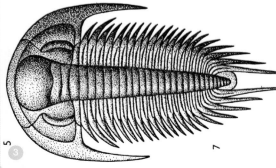

although those with a keen eye may encounter the unremarkable tracks and trails of soft-bodied, anonymous creatures who tunnelled their way through the sea-floor sand in search of tasty titbits. Later, however, the muddy Cambrian sea floor was positively crawling with life, a fact dramatically brought to the attention of Fellows of the Geological Society of London in 1863 by John William Salter, a palaeontologist employed by the Geological Survey: 'My object now', he explained in measured tones, 'is to point out the locality and geological place of a giant Trilobite long looked for in Britain ...' The place was Porth-y-rhaw, a secluded bay halfway between Caerbwdi Bay and Solfa. The trilobite – one of the most instantly recognizable of all fossils – that he discovered in the blue-black mudstones proved to be a fifteen-centimetre long monster christened *Paradoxides davidis*, not in honour of St David but rather in recognition of Salter's geological friend, David Homfray of Porthmadog. News of the discovery prompted geological pilgrims in their droves to head west but, like Salter, those lucky enough to find any

1. *Porth Lisgi: varicoloured tuffs;*
2. *Clegyr Boia; 3. Carreg Frân*

signs of the ancient crustaceans, that swarmed in the Cambrian seas, had to be content with fragments, for the layers of splintery mudstones, tipped on end by powerful forces within the Earth's crust, are so shot through with cracks and fractures that they readily break into innumerable small pieces. Paradoxically, diminutive blind trilobites, no more than a few millimetres in length, have survived the vicissitudes of 500 million years of entombment and are to be found intact – for those armed with a good hand lens! – alongside the fragmentary remains of the giant *Paradoxides*.

Curiously enough, serendipity played its part in Salter's exciting discovery. It seems as though he had intended to land his boat at Solfa, the sheltered tidal harbour which, like Porth Clais and the smaller inlet of Porth-y-rhaw, also lies at the seaward end of a large glacial meltwater channel whose lower reaches were drowned by the post-glacial rise in sea level. But a visit to Solfa may well have been equally rewarding, for the dark mudstones in the cliff behind what is now the old Lifeboat House, built on Trinity Quay seven years after Salter's visit to Pembrokeshire in 1862, also once yielded fragments of *Paradoxides*.

Although the youngest Cambrian rocks are exposed in the cliffs a little short of the bounding headlands of Solfa harbour, they are best seen at Trwynhwrddyn, the low headland on the north side of Porth Mawr (Whitesands Bay) from where St Patrick is said to have set sail to Ireland. Here, in the so-called Lingula Flags, the tongue-shaped fossil sea shell *Lingulella* is relatively common on the surfaces of some of the folded layers of shallow-water sandstones and mudstones. If you then head south along the Coast Path from Porth Mawr to the small Iron Age promontory fort of Castell Heinif, situated beyond the St David's Lifeboat Station at Porth Stinan, you will discover that the sequence of Cambrian rocks encountered between Solfa and Porth Clais is repeated. Here, too, the strata plunges steeply seawards, for both sequences are part of a huge up-fold or anticline, whose axis, aligned approximately east-north-east–west-south-west, runs through the very centre of the St David's peninsula. Those rocks occupying the core of the beheaded anticline are not only very different to the sedimentary and fossil-bearing strata of Cambrian age but are also amongst the oldest in Wales.

Along that section of the Coast Path south of Castell Heinif, around the headland of Pen Dal-aderyn and on as far as Porth Lisgi, the 'core' rocks underfoot are part of a thick pile of volcanic ash (tuffs) and lava flows varying in character, hardness and colour, and all intensely altered. Grey green and purple tuffs are widespread around the headland but, at Porth Lisgi, hard buff- and dull-purple-coloured tuffs and angular volcanic rubble (agglomerate) occur alongside soft multicoloured tuffs. At nearby Clegyr Boia (Clegyrfwya), on the other hand, one of several small, rocky 'islands' that rise above the coastal plateau planed across the St David's peninsula perhaps as recently as five million years ago, the tuffs are green in colour and extremely hard. The colour is most apt, for legend has it that Clegyr Boia, which is known to have been the site of a Neolithic settlement and later Iron Age encampment, was the home of Boia, an intractable chieftain and druid who hailed from the Emerald Isle! A thorn in the flesh of the saintly Dewi, Boia was eventually killed by Lisgi, a fellow Irishman.

Long after the lavas and tuffs were formed, molten magma welled up into the huge stack of volcanic rocks and there slowly cooled and crystallized in a subterranean chamber, deep within the Earth's crust, to form an extremely hard, light grey granitic rock, called granophyre. Its hardness and resistance to wave attack accounts for the fact that the 587 million-year-old rock, formed over 40 million years before the beginning of Cambrian times, is the foundation of the twin islets of Carreg Frân and Carreg yr Esgob, both dismembered but stubbornly unyielding fragments of the prominent headland east of Porth Lisgi.

The first person to recognize that the St David's granophyre and the associated older tuffs and lavas were of Precambrian age was Henry Hicks, born in St David's in 1837. Although a doctor by profession, who had looked after the medical needs of the families of his home village between 1862 and 1871, Hicks was also a very gifted and accomplished amateur geologist. But by advocating the presence in Pembrokeshire of rocks of Precambrian age, a concept which the professional geologists of the Geological Survey of Great Britain did not entertain at the time, he fell foul of the geological 'establishment' and became embroiled in one of the greatest controversies in the history of British geology. In meetings of the Geological Society of London, held in the spring of 1883, Archibald Geikie, then Director of the Geological Survey, spearheaded a vitriolic attack on Hicks' work. As a parting shot at the close of the second confrontational meeting, Geikie patronizingly expressed the hope that 'Dr Hicks and himself would continue friends, and that the time would come when they would go over the ground together neither believing in the existence of Precambrian rocks'! As it transpired it was a vain hope. Hicks, the amateur and latter-day 'David' of St David's, who in 1885 was elected FRS in recognition of his geological research work and had served as President of the Geological Society of London during 1896–8, had the satisfaction of knowing before his untimely death in 1899 that he had slain the geological 'Goliath' following officialdom's acceptance of the existence of rocks of Precambrian age!

During his time in St David's, Dr Henry Hicks, a Welsh-speaking Welshman blessed with a fine singing voice, was also called upon to take part in concerts held in the City Hall to raise money towards swelling the coffers of the fund that had been established to pay for the restoration of the cathedral, under the guidance of George Gilbert Scott. And given his interest in the project, the nature of the building stones would surely not have escaped his geological gaze. Unlike the west wall, which was then being rebuilt with blocks of Caerbwdi sandstone, the entire rubble walls were built almost exclusively of Precambrian tuffs, the bulk of which came from quarries dug into the flanks of Glyn Rhosyn, within a stone's throw of the building. Indeed, the gritty purple tuffs exposed in the Penrhiw quarry near Pontypenyd, about 400 metres north of the cathedral, have often been mistaken for Caerbwdi sandstone, a fact which has led some to claim erroneously that the building's exterior walls were constructed largely, if not wholly, of the plum-coloured sandstone. The rubble walls of St Mary's College, adjoining the cathedral, Porth y Tŵr and the Bishop's Palace, are also largely built of the same locally-quarried tuffs, whose present condition leaves

1. Dr Henry Hicks' memorial tablet, Hendon Parish Church; 2. Purple Cambrian tuff, often wrongly identified as Caerbwdi sandstone; 3. St David's Cathedral: glacial erratics, including Carn Llidi gabbro, in wall of south transept

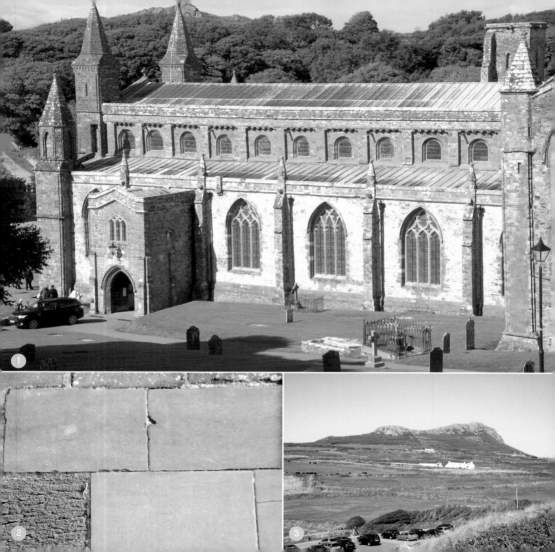

much to be desired. Many of the soft pink, yellow, buff, brown and light green tuffs in particular are badly pitted and disintegrate at the merest touch. So, in an attempt to arrest the weathering of the tuffs, a section of the exterior rubble wall between the south porch and south transept has been given a coating of lime mortar, a practice widely used during the Middle Ages but somewhat frustrating in the eyes of present-day geologists eager to ascertain the nature and provenance of building stones.

The only building stones that have survived the onslaught of salt-laden winds are the hard purple tuffs and green tuffs, together with several 'foreign' boulders, such as those set in the exterior wall of the cathedral's south transept. Dumped during the retreat of the Irish Sea ice-sheet that overwhelmed the peninsula some 20,000 years ago, most of the boulders were plucked from the craggy slopes of Carn Llidi and Penbiri, both summits being part and parcel of one of several thick sheets of a hard, dark-coloured igneous rock (gabbro) injected into soft mudstones of Ordovician age. This was a period when volcanic activity, so much a feature of the Precambrian landscape, re-established itself with a vengeance. So much so, that almost every headland along the north coast of the St David's peninsula between St David's Head (Penmaendewi) and the former stone-quarrying, slate-quarrying and brick-making village of Porth-gain, is of resistant Ordovician igneous rock, whilst every bay is carved in softer sedimentary strata of the same age.

1. St David's Cathedral: lime-washed exterior wall of nave; 2. Blocks of unweathered Caerbwdi sandstone: west wall of St David's Cathedral; 3. Carn Llidi © Gwasg Carreg Gwalch

3. The Harlech Dome and Snowdonia's 'Ring of Fire'

Cambrian [543–490 million years ago] –
Ordovician [490–443 million years ago]

West of the A470 road between Dolgellau and Trawsfynydd, stretch the undulating skyline of Y Rhinogydd, a tract of wild uplands and dark naked rocks, thickly mantled with heather and block scree. As a consequence, their isolated and inhospitable summits – Diffwys (750 m), Y Llethr (754 m), Rhinog Fach (711 m), Rhinog Fawr (720 m) and Moel Ysgyfarnogod (623 m) – are *terra incognita* to all but the most venturesome walkers and the resident population of feral goats. The *c.*530 million-year-old rocks – mainly coarse-grained sandstones (grits) – forming the foundation of the entire tract of land west of the main road and the coastline between the Glaslyn–Dwyryd estuary in the north and the Mawddach

1. *Y Rhinogydd*; 2. *Harlech Castle*

© Gwasg Carreg Gwalch

estuary in the south are of Cambrian age and because they are in the form of an upturned saucer the entire area is known as the Harlech Dome. It's by far the most impressive and most extensive outcrop of Cambrian rocks in Wales and for less energetic walkers there's no better place to examine the layers of grit than the rocky promontory on which stands Harlech Castle, one of several colossal fortresses built by Edward I around the mountain mass of Snowdonia (Eryri) to suppress the

1. Rhinog Fawr; 2. Graded layers of gritstone; 3. National Botanic Garden of Wales: slabs of purple Cambrian slate

Welsh. Indeed, most of the imposing castle over-looking the vast expanse of Morfa Harlech is built of local Rhinog Grit, which, along with Barmouth Grit and an earlier succession of mudstones (destined to be compressed into slate during a period of mountain building about 410 million years ago and intermittently mined in vast underground caverns near Llanfair, south of Harlech, between c.1860 and the First World War),

Adam Sedgwick

Roderick Impey Murchison

originally accumulated in the so-called Welsh Basin, a repository of marine sediments that persisted throughout the greater part of Cambrian, Ordovician and Silurian times.

Viewed from the pass of Bwlch Tyddiad, reached via the Roman Steps (a roughly paved footpath never once trodden by disgruntled Roman legionnaires) that head south-east from the delightful Llyn Cwm Bychan, the north face of Rhinog Fawr is a sight to behold. There, according to Andrew Crombie

Ramsay, author of *The Geology of North Wales* (1866, 1881), the eye is drawn to layer upon layer of westward-tilted grit that rise in terrace-like steps, presenting energetic walkers with 'one of the grandest spectacles, both geologically and as a piece of rugged scenery that North Wales affords'. An examination of an individual layer (bed) of grit invariably reveals that the size of the sand grains decreases progressively upwards, with the finest-grained material at the top of the bed. Such a repetative pattern indicates that the grits were formed as submarine fans, fed by powerful gravity-driven, sediment-laden currents which, on reaching the sea floor, initially deposited their load of coarse-grained sand, followed by finer-grained material as the currents lost momentum.

Although the Cambrian rocks in the Bethesda-Llanberis-Nantlle region are of similar age to the grits of the Harlech Dome, they are mostly mudstones, later transformed into purple and green slates of the Gwynedd slate belt, famous for their ability to cleave into thin layers to form unrivalled roofing slates. Indeed, that transformation took place about 80 million years or more after the deposition of the fine-grained mud that had accumulated in the Welsh Basin, situated along the south-eastern flank of the ancient Iapetus Ocean, which separated most of present-day Europe from North America. But the relatively undisturbed, watery world of the Welsh Basin in Cambrian times was soon to be rudely interrupted by intense volcanic activity that characterized the 47 million-year-long history of the succeeding Ordovician, a period of which there is no mention in Ramsay's *The Geology of North Wales*.

In 1835, forty-six years prior to the publication of the second edition of Ramsay's hugely influential book in 1881, Adam Sedgwick, Professor of Geology at Oxford, and Roderick Impey Murchison, who was appointed Director General of the Geological Survey of Great Britain in 1855, presented a joint paper to the British Association for the Advancement of Science that led to the recognition of two geological systems. Both were given names with Welsh associations: the Cambrian after Cambria, the Latin for Wales; and the Silurian after the Silures, an Iron Age tribe occupying what is now south-east Wales. However, as a consequence of the then ill-defined boundary between the two systems, the two erstwhile friends became sworn enemies. The bitter struggle was not resolved until 1879 when Charles Lapworth, prior to his appointment as Professor of Geology at Birmingham University, correctly argued that a succession of rocks considered to be Lower Silurian by Murchison and to be Upper Cambrian by Sedgwick could, on the basis of their fossil content, be regarded as a separate system. The

1. *Cadair Idris; 2. Moelwyn Bach–Moelwyn Mawr; 3. Rhobell Fawr*

Rocks of Wales

Ordovician – named after the Ordovices, an Iron Age tribe based in north-west Wales – was duly recognized but not by all. Such was the influence of Murchison's work, that the term Ordovician did not appear on the maps of the Geological Survey until 1906. Furthermore, as a conseqence of its recognition, the territory occupied by Cambrian rocks was but a mere fraction of what Sedgwick had always demanded.

A scramble to the summit of Rhinog Fawr, a kilometre south of Bwlch Tyddiad, is well worth the effort, for the boldness and rugged grandeur of the north Wales mountains that border the Cambrian rocks to the south, east and north of the Harlech Dome, is attributable in large measure to extensive outcrops of resistant Ordovician igneous rocks interspersed among the marine sediments accumulating within the Welsh Basin. From south to north, the panorama encompasses Penygadair (Cadair Idris; 893 m), Aran Fawddwy (905 m) and Aran Benllyn (885 m), Rhobell Fawr (734 m), Arennig Fawr (854 m), Moelwyn Mawr

1. Aran Fawddwy; 2. Near Pont Gethin: a roadside (A470) exposure of welded tuffs; 3. Tyrrau Mawr (Craig-las)

(770 m), Carnedd Llywelyn (1,064 m), Glyder Fawr (999 m) and Snowdon (Yr Wyddfa; 1085 m), all of which were the centres of volcanic activity at sometime or other between 490 million years and 440 million years ago. The volcanicity developed as the dense oceanic plate forming part of the floor of the ancient Iapetus Ocean, that lay between the equally ancient continents of Laurentia ('North America') and Avalonia-Baltica ('Europe'), was forced down (subducted) under the thicker and less dense Avalonian plate. Partial melting of the oceanic plate led to the formation of magma (molten rock) which, being lighter, ascended through the overlying crust, leading to the formation of volcanoes if the magma reached the surface, or intrusions of igneous rock if the molten rock cooled and crystallized deep within the Earth's crust.

The earliest eruptions were centred upon Rhobell Fawr, the remote dome-shaped summit north-east of Dolgellau, which consists of numerous sheets of dark basaltic lava spewed out from a volcanic island-based volcano about 490 million years ago. In all probability the volcanic episodes here and elsewhere along Snowdonia's incomplete 'Ring of Fire'

were short-lived and for far longer periods of time the volcanoes on volcanic islands and the sea floor lay dormant.

In contrast to the 4,000 metre thick succession of basaltic lava that are the eroded remnants of the Rhobell Fawr volcano, the vast majority of the volcanic rocks are complex sequences of tuffs (hardened volcanic ash), welded tuffs (often called ash-flow tuffs, that is, incandescent, ashy clouds that retained sufficient heat on deposition for the constituent material to adhere to produce a lava-like rock, often streaky in appearance), lava flows (which together with tuffs and welded tuffs that may have accumulated either on the Earth's surface or on the sea floor) and igneous intrusions (bodies of igneous rocks formed as a result of the crystallization of magma thrust amidst pre-existing rocks).

With the passage of time the volcanicity that began in the earliest Tremadog epoch of Ordovician times continued unabated into the succeeding Arennig, Llanvirn (Llan-fyrn) and Llandeilo epochs. The 490–455 million-year-old volcanic rocks, the product of violent eruptions capable of blasting skywards huge ash clouds (eruption

1. Crib Goch; 2. Pitt's Head (Cerrig Collwyn); 3. Fossil sea shell in ash-flow tuffs; Clogwyn y Geifr opposite Yr Wyddfa and Y Lliwedd

plumes) mixed with hot gases to heights in excess of 10,000 metres, underpin the imposing summits of Arennig Fawr, Aran Fawddwy–Aran Benllyn and Cadair Idris, on whose apex are piles of pillow lavas, formed as a result of the submarine eruption of basaltic lava. The spectacular cliffs of Tyrrau Mawr (Craig-las) at the western end of the dramatic north-facing escarpment of Cadair Idris are attributable to the presence of a thick sheet of granitic rock intruded into slightly older less resistant volcanic rocks and mudstones.

But it was during the succeeding Caradoc (Caradog) epoch, 455 to 446 million years ago, that Ordovician volcanism reached its climax. Indeed, Snowdon – one of the 'Seven Wonders of Wales' – and its adjoing summits, together with Y Glyderau and Y Carneddau, are largely carved from volcanic rocks of Caradog age. Two major rock sequences have been identified: the Llywelyn Volcanic Group, centered upon Y Carneddau, east of the A5 between Capel Curig and Bethesda, and west of the Conwy valley (Dyffryn Conwy), and the Snowdon Volcanic Group of central Snowdonia. The two centres are separated one from another by a thick unit of marine mudstones and siltstones of the so-called

Cwm Eigiau Formation that represent a period of relative volcanic calm.

The Llywelyn Group largely consists of an enormously thick succession of lavas and ash-flow tuffs, the product of major submarine and land-based volcanic eruptions, in addition to layers of sandstone, siltstone and mudstone deposited on the floor of a shallow sea. In contrast, the rocks of the Snowdon Group are more varied and comprise – in association with marine sedimentary rocks – ash-flow tuffs, tuffs, basaltic and rhyolitic lava. (Rhyolite, the fine-grained equivalent of granite, white, grey or reddish in colour, underpins Crib Goch [red ridge], an awesome arête sculpted by an 'ice age' glacier that offers the most challenging route to Snowdon summit.) The cataclysmic eruptions of the Snowdon Group were heralded by the formation of the Pitt's Head Tuff, named after Cerrig Collwyn, a distinctive outcrop of ash-flow tuff alongside the A4085 between Beddgelert and Rhyd-ddu, whose profile is said to resemble the head of William Pitt the Younger (1759–1806)! Despite the ferocity of the eruptions, some of Snowdon's tuffs were the product of volcanic ash-falls that accumulated on the sea floor, where life flourished during quiescent interludes. Just below the summit platform well-bedded tuffs actually contain fossil sea shells, proof positive that the mountain's very apex once formed part of an ancient seabed. That said, even the most keen-eyed budding geologist would do well to spot them amongst the feet of countless visitors, jostling to set foot on Snowdon's highest point!

No less unexpected than the fossil sea shells are the remains of the Snowdon copper mine above the shores of Glaslyn at the foot of the summit. In fact, it is one of about 30 relatively small copper mines that were at their most productive during the nineteenth century, although many, such as Sygun, now a visitor attraction near Beddgelert, were unprofitable ventures. (Established c.1830 but abandoned in 1903, the old Sygun mine was, for a brief period, the unlikely location of a 'Chinese town' during the filming of the Ingrid Bergman, *Inn of the Sixth Happiness* [1958])! All the mines, whose chequered histories have been recorded in considerable detail by David

1. *Glaslyn; 2. The derelict Gwynfynydd gold-mine; 3. Cwm Idwal–Twll Du*

Bick in his book entitled *The Old Copper Mines of Snowdonia* (1982), were intimately associated with the igneous rocks of the Snowdon Volcanic Group, whose hot mineralizing fluids gave rise to copper-bearing mineral veins that permeated faults and cracks within the rocks. In the Harlech Dome a similar number of ventures were actively involved in the mining of manganese ores, whereas over 20 gold-mines of the so-called Dolgellau Gold Belt, were at the peak of production between 1900 and 1905. In 1904, the famous Clogau mine, located a short distance north of Bont-ddu on the shores of the Mawddach estuary, produced 18,417 ounces of gold, valued at £66,000. In all, over 81,000 ounces of gold were won from this mine alone! Clogau's only rival was Gwynfynydd, situated on the banks of Afon Mawddach, easily accessible via a short three-kilometre-walk north of Y Ganllwyd on the Dolgellau-Trawsfynydd road. Rhaeadr Mawddach, the waterfall immediately upstream of the river's confluence with Afon Gain (a stone's throw from the elegant fall of Pistyll Cain), provided power to drive the processing machinery of the Gwynfynydd gold-mine, which included an enormous waterwheel (later replaced by a powerful turbine) and stone-crusher. The mine's best year was 1888 when in excess of 8,700 ounces of gold, valued at £27,300, were extracted from almost 4,000 tonnes of useless crushed quartz, which together with lesser quantities of pyrite, sphalerite (zinc ore) and galena (lead ore) accounted for the bulk of the gold-bearing veins that cut through black mudstones of Cambrian age. In total, the gold-mines of the Dolgellau Gold Belt yielded a staggering 130,000 ounces of the precious metal but none are currently working.

As a consequence of the inexorable movement of Earth's tectonic plates, the two ancient continents of Laurentia and Avalonia-Baltica, that once lay on opposite shores of the Iapetus Ocean, collided about 410 million years ago. The momentous collision led to the cessation of the volcanicity, that had been the hallmark of Ordovician times, and mountain building on a grand scale. Furthermore, the formation of the Caledonian Mountain chain of Himalayan proportions, traceable from Scandinavia, via northern Britain, to the northern Appalachians of North America, resulted in the deformation of rocks not only of

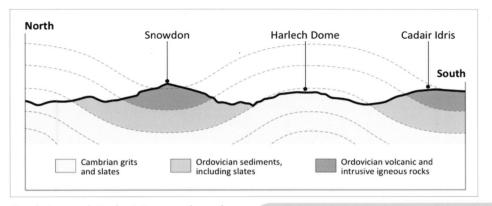

Cambrian and Ordovician age but also those of Silurian age. Though mere eroded remnants of the once mighty Caledonides, Snowdonia's rock succession retains the indelible imprint of complex folds and fractures that bear testimony to the enormous compressive forces generated as the jaws of the gigantic tectonic vice between the colliding continents gradually closed over a period of many millions of years. Though not easily appreciated in the field, by far the largest and most impressive fold is that centred upon the Harlech Dome, whose eroded remains are overlooked by the towering north-facing Cadair Idris escarpment to the south and the imposing Snowdon massif to the

Snowdon–Harlech Dome–Cadair Idris: a generalized cross-section

north. In contrast, the spectacular downfold known as the Snowdon syncline is clearly to be seen in the north-east facing craggy cliffs immediately below the summit of Snowdon; in Clogwyn Du'r Arddu, which has long been celebrated by rock-climbers as the finest of British cliffs; and in the ramparts of Clogwyn y Geifr at the back of Cwm Idwal, where generations of apprentice rock-climbers have honed their skills on the Idwal Slabs (Rhiwiau Caws), thick layers of ash-flow tuffs forming part of the syncline's south-eastern limb.

4. Rocks of the Welsh Basin: Cardigan Bay and the Elenydd Mountains

Ordovician [490–443 million years ago] – Silurian [443–417 million years ago]

On a slight rise in the middle of a field known as Parc Carreg-y-lluniau ('the field of the illustrated stone'), about a kilometre east of Tre-saith on the shores of Cardigan Bay (Bae Ceredigion), stands a rough, unshaped, quad-rangular pillar of weathered sandstone bearing the Latin inscription '*Corbalengi iacit/ Ordovs*' (Of Corbalengus, [here] he lies, an Ordovician). The stone was first described in 1695 by the Shropshire-born Welshman, Edward Llwyd (Lhuyd), keeper of the Ashmolean Museum in Oxford, and it was he who was the first to link '*Ordovs*' with the Ordovices, which at the

1. *Weathered sandstone pillar commemorating Corbalengus;*
2. *An unweathered slate slab of Cambrian age; cemetery of derelict Church of the Holy Cross, Llechryd*

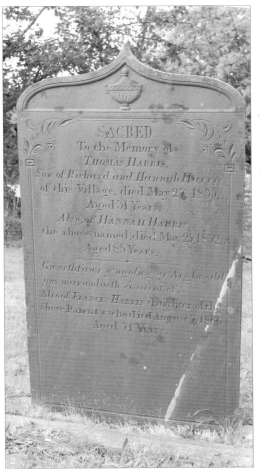

SACRED
To the Memory of
THOMAS HARRIS,
Son of Richard and Hannah Harris
of this Village, died May 27, 1835,
Aged 34 Years
Also, of HANNAH HARRIS
the above named, died May 25, 1852,
Aged 85 Years.

Gweithfawr yngolwg yr Arglwydd
yw marwolaeth ei saint &c.
Also of FRANCES HARRIS daughter of the
above Parents who died August 1, 1846,
Aged 71 Years.

time of the Roman conquest controlled considerable areas of northern and central Wales. Both the Ordovices and the Silures – the Iron Age tribe occupying much of south-east Wales and who provided the most implacable resistance to Roman expansion of any of the other British tribes – were destined to be immortalized by nineteenth-century geologists eager to define and name two early chapters in the Earth's long history: Ordovician and Silurian. But what Llwyd would not have appreciated is that Corbalengus, the hapless Ordovician who had strayed into the tribal lands of the Demetae of south-west Wales, was buried in a grave marked by a block of local Silurian sandstone, a stone's throw from the nearest outcrop of Ordovician rock – home ground, geologically speaking, but foreign soil in reality!

Just visible from the commemorative stone is the double-bellcote and white-washed walls of St Michael's Church, Penbryn. So too is its distinctive purple-slated roof. The slates, together with the purple grave slabs erected in the circular churchyard, were fashioned from large blocks of high-quality slate hewn in the vast Penrhyn, Dinorwig or Nantlle quarries of the Cambrian slate belt of north-west Wales. Both the imported slates and gravestones, probably came via nearby Llangrannog, one of several bustling centres of shipbuilding and seafaring activity that were a feature of the Cardigan Bay (Bae Ceredigion) coast throughout the nineteenth century. Also imported were most of the grey-blue slate gravestones, the product of the small, but locally important, Fforest and Cilgerran quarries situated on the banks of the river Teifi between Cardigan (Aberteifi) and Llechryd.

About 30 million years after having first accumulated as layers of mud on the sea floor towards the end of Ordovician times – some 440 million years ago – these slates were formed as powerful earth movements squeezed and folded the ancient mudstones. Although incredibly intense, nowhere was the pressure sufficient to transform the mudstones into high quality slates to rival those of north Wales. Being softer and less easily split into thin sheets, roofing slates were more difficult to make and hence the Teifi-side quarries concentrated on the production of window sills, doorsteps, hearthstones and gravestones, in addition to the squared oblong slabs and rough hewn blocks and rubble which formed the bulk of the building stones used by local stonemasons in the small towns and villages north and south of the lower Teifi valley.

Alternate courses of local slate slabs and blocks of Ordovician sandstone are a striking feature of portions of the ruined walls of St Dogmael's Abbey (Abaty Llandudoch), established on the south bank of the Teifi estuary in the early twelfth century by monks from the mother abbey of Tiron in France. This pattern was subsequently adopted by local stonemasons, for attractively banded late eighteenth to early twentieth-century cottages, terraced houses, town houses, chapels and riverside warehouses and industrial premises are a common local peculiarity and unique aspect of the built heritage of both the village of St Dogmael's and nearby Cardigan town.

As far as Llangrannog, about 15 kilometres north-east of Cardigan, folded and fractured layers of slaty mudstones and associated sandstones, magnificently exposed in the coastal cliffs, are of Ordovician age. North of the village,

1. St Dogmael's Abbey: banded stonework;
2. Cottage, St Dogmael's: banded stonework

however, the rocks of the coastal cliffs as far north as the Dyfi estuary, and the bulk of those of inland Ceredigion and the Elenydd mountains – the 'massif central' of mid Wales – are of Silurian age. Locally, and especially amongst those with an interest in matters literary and maritime, Llangrannog is famous as the birthplace and resting place of the redoubtable Sarah Jane Rees (1839–1916), better known as Cranogwen: schoolteacher; preacher and lecturer; founder of a local school at which basic navigational skills were taught; editor of *Y Frythones* (a Welsh-language women's magazine) and founder of a women's temperance movement.

The Silurian rocks record the same style of sedimentation as had been established during Ordovician times. The monotonous alternation of layers of mudstones and sandstones – once compared to 'a club sandwich stacked to infinity' – were deposited in the deep water of the Welsh Basin, a huge repository of mud and sand on the north-western margin of the long-lost ancient continent of Avalonia, that then lay about 30° south of the Equator. Beyond the

Folded Aberystwyth Grits, Traeth Pen-y-graig, a superb example of a syncline

shoreline of Avalonia – traceable from the Welsh borderlands near Welshpool (Y Trallwng), to Rhayader (Rhaeadr Gwy), Llandovery (Llanymddyfri) and on to Haverfordwest (Hwlffordd) – a steep continental slope, scarred by submarine canyons, separated a shallow, continental-shelf sea on the margins of the so-called Midland Platform to the east and south from a deep ocean floor to the north-west.

On the shelf, rivers deposited vast quantities of soft, unstable mud, silt and sand which, when disturbed by the violent vibrations of periodic earthquakes, would slide, slump and ultimately flow, often at great speed, down the continental slope and into the deep basin in the form of dense, turbulent clouds of sediment called turbidity currents. A modern example of one of these great sediment flows was triggered by the Grand Banks earthquake of 1929, whose epicentre lay off the southern coast of Newfoundland. As the sediment-laden current accelerated down offshore canyons – themselves initiated and deepened by successive flows – towards the deep ocean, it tore through twelve submarine telegraph cables, snapping them in at least twenty-three places. Though short-lived, such powerful erosive currents are also effective agents of deposition, for at the base of the continental slope their speed rapidly decreases, prompting them to dump their load of sand and mud in the form of huge fans or lobes at the mouths of the submarine canyons.

Take a journey from Cwmtydu, south-west of New Quay (Ceinewydd), to Y Borth north of Aberystwyth – a distance of about 36 kilometres as the crow flies – and you can trace not only one of the first group of rocks to have been identified as the deposits of deep-water turbidity currents, but also find one of the finest examples of a turbidite sequence in Britain. Called the Aberystwyth Grits, magnificently exposed in the coastal cliffs of Cardigan Bay, the sequence is composed of alternating layers of grey sandstone and dark blue-grey mudstone, each couplet the result of one turbid flow; coarse sand being deposited first, followed by finer silt and mud as the flow begins to reduce speed. And because the numerous pulses of sediment that flowed into the basin came via a submarine canyon located some distance south-west of Cwmtydu, the couplets of sandstone and mudstone become progressively thinner and finer-grained when traced northwards, away from the mouth of the canyon.

Go to New Quay, not far removed from the mouth of the canyon, and you will find that the rock sequence is dominated by thick layers of coarse-grained sandstone separated by thin bands of siltstone and mudstone. But between Aberystwyth and Y Borth, at the northern extremity of the submarine fan radiating from the canyon mouth, the turbidity currents were much weaker and as a consequence the turbidites are thin and fine-grained.

For a closer look at rocks typical of the Aberystwyth Grits, take a stroll to the north end of the promenade at Aberystwyth – 'kick the bar [the railing at the far end of the prom] once for a degree and twice for a partner', in the time-honoured fashion of Aberystwyth University students – and examine the outcrops near the foot of Constitution Hill. On the underside of many of the layers of sandstone, are bulbous, tongue-shaped, protuberances called flute casts, formed by sand infilling hollows in the

1. Craig y Delyn, near Y Borth; © David Evans
2. Flute casts, St Michael's Church, Llanfihangel-y-Creuddyn; 3. Early Silurian graptolites

underlying mudstone scoured out by eddies as the currents flowed across a muddy sea floor. Flutes are typically asymmetrical in shape, with steep bulbous noses pointing up-current. They are therefore excellent indicators of the direction of flow of the currents that deposited the turbidites and in the case of the Aberystwyth Grits they indicate that the currents flowed from south to north.

Curious meandering tracks, known as trace fossils, created by the crawling or feeding activity of anonymous worm-like sea creatures, are also commonly preserved as casts on the underside of sandstone beds. But disappointment awaits those in search of 'real' fossils. Graptolites, floating colonial organisms that swarmed in the surface waters of the Silurian seas and are, in places, found covering the surfaces of successive layers of mudstone with what look like miniature hacksaw blades are notoriously difficult to find in the Aberystwyth Grits. Generally incapable of withstanding and surviving the short-lived and fast-moving turbid

slurries of sediment that poured into the Welsh Basin, the delicate remains of these planktonic creatures are best preserved in the thin layers of mudstone that record the gentle rain of very fine-grained mud that settled on the sea floor between the more violent episodes. In the Rheidol gorge near Ponterwyd, for instance, stick-like graptolite colonies preserved in brassy iron pyrites have been recovered from the mudstones by keen-eyed palaeontologists.

About 12 kilometres south of Ponterwyd, the Hendre quarry at Ystradmeurig has exploited the Ystradmeurig Grits, a mass of coarse-grained grey sandstones containing occasional layers of pebbles. The rocks hereabouts represent a lobe of another submarine fan, but unlike the younger Aberystwyth Grits, flute casts and other marks on the undersurface of sandstone layers indicate that the deposits in this case flooded into the Welsh Basin from an easterly direction via another submarine canyon. The source of this so-called Caban Canyon lay near the present site of Caban-coch, one of four reservoirs established in the narrow, gorge-like Elan valley west of Rhayader during the 1890s and 1900s to supply water to Birmingham. Although many of the hand-chiselled

1. Folded Aberystwyth Grits, Traeth Pen-y-graig; 2. The Ystradmeurig Grits, Hendre Quarry, Ystradmeurig; 3. Caban-coch Conglomerate, Cwm Elan

1. The coastal plateau north of Llanrhystud;
2. Abandoned buildings and waste tips,
Cwmystwyth mine

facing stones of the dam walls of all four reservoirs are blocks of Carboniferous Pennant sandstone from the Craig yr Hesg quarry near Pontypridd, in the centre of the south Wales coalfield, the bulk of the stone used in their construction was obtained from Chwarel y Gigfran, the quarry at the northern end of the Caban-coch dam wall. The remarkable coarse conglomerates – rocks packed full of rounded pebbles and cobbles – and sandstones exposed in the quarry and nearby crags, were deposited in channels within the upper reaches of the Caban Canyon, by extremely powerful, north-westerly-flowing turbidity currents. In contrast, the sand and smaller pebbles that had accumulated on the continental shelf to the east, were swept down the Caban Canyon and out into the deep Welsh Basin beyond, thereby building up the Ystradmeurig submarine fan.

As the end of Silurian times drew ever closer, the days of the Welsh Basin were increasingly numbered. Over a period of many millions of years the two continents of Avalonia and Laurentia, separated by the Iapetus Ocean, had been edging ever closer to one another at a rate of a few centimetres a year. They finally locked horns about 410 million years ago – a stupendous continental collision that resulted in the creation of the mighty Caledonian mountain chain, traceable from Spitsbergen, bordering the Arctic Ocean, to the southern Appalachians. Incorporated within that mountain chain were not only the crumpled, folded and fractured piles of Cambrian, Ordovician and Silurian sedimentary rocks that had accumulated within the Welsh Basin, but also igneous rocks which, with few exceptions, were the product of Ordovician volcanicity.

As a result of the mighty collision between Avalonia and Laurentia, most of the Ordovician and Silurian rocks of the area were crunched up along east-north-east–west-south-west belts, a geological 'grain' reflected in the outline of Cardigan Bay and the trend of the middle reaches of the Tywi and Teifi valleys that mirror the course of two great up-folds that formed at this time: the Tywi and Teifi anticlines. But even though erosion has exploited some major lines of geological weakness, the long and remarkably level skylines of the Elenydd mountains, traceable from Pumlumon in the north to Llandovery in the south, and from Tregaron in the west to Llanwrtyd in the east, are as spectacularly indifferent to the pattern of folds in the underlying rocks as are the coastal plateaux of Ceredigion and neighbouring Pembrokeshire.

Nowhere are the seemingly endless stretches of Elenydd's gently undulating and desolate moorlands more apparent than on the summit of Pumlumon, that stands on the crest of the Teifi Anticline, whose core is marked by an outcrop of Ordovician rocks. Had it not been for the sunshine that greeted him on reaching the summit, George Borrow – enthusiastic traveller, eccentric and author of *Wild Wales* (1862) – found the vista of treeless moorland and peat bog 'cheerless in the extreme'! It's here too, from oozings out of blanket peat, that the rivers Severn (Hafren) and Wye (Gwy) head south-east and the Rheidol south-west, the latter from its source in Llyn Llygad Rheidol, a small cirque lake that nestles below Pen Pumlumon Fawr (752 metres; the highest of the five alleged peaks of Pumlumon).

Fractures formed during the uplift of

the Caledonian mountains, and repeatedly reactivated and added to during later phases of stress caused by the perpetual motion of tectonic plates, have imposed an indelible imprint on the human landscape of northern Ceredigion and neighbouring parts of Powys. Strung like beads along east-north-east–west-south-west trending fault lines are the remains of over 130 lead, zinc and copper mines. The exploitation of metalliferous ores, precipitated from hot mineral-rich fluids that periodically invaded the lines of weakness over a period of many millions of years, has a long history. Mining at Cwmystwyth dates back to the Bronze Age but it reached its peak in the middle of the nineteenth century. Since 1845, when it became compulsory to keep records, the Central Wales Orefield is known to have produced over 440,000 tonnes of lead ore, almost 140,000 tonnes of zinc ore and in excess of more than 7,800 tonnes of copper ore, in addition to a staggering 2,500,000 ounces (one ounce = 28.35 grams) or more of silver.

In the deeply-entrenched, secluded valleys north of the now busy A44 road, between Aberystwyth and Ponterwyd, the mines of Cwmsymlog, Cwmerfyn and

1. *Aberystwyth Castle;* 2. *Cwmsymlog mine;*
3. *Ruined buildings and waste tips, Wemyss mine, near Fron-goch mine*

Rocks of Wales

Goginan were famed for their silver production. Until 1637 the valuable metal was despatched to the Tower mint in London, but because this practice was both expensive and dangerous, Thomas Bushell, lessee of the Royal Mines in Wales, sought permission to open a mint in Aberystwyth. His request was granted and the mint, which was in operation between 1639 and 1642, was established in the grounds of the grey sandstone and mudstone walls of Aberystwyth Castle (originally completed on behalf of Edward I in 1289 but much decayed by the middle of the sixteenth century). In contrast to the mint's short life, Cwmsymlog mine, according to one mid eighteenth-century observer, remained 'the richest in lead and silver of any of His Majesty's dominions'.

Bonanzas, though few and far between, were not unknown. Over a period of four months between November 1826 and March 1827 over 13,000 tonnes of lead ore were raised at the ancient Cwmystwyth mine. Tucked away in the hills between the Ystwyth and Rheidol valleys south-west of Devil's Bridge (Pontarfynach), Fron-goch mine, easily the most productive mine in

Outflow of polluted water, Cwmystwyth mine

Ceredigion, yielded over 50,000 tonnes of zinc ore, in addition to several thousand tonnes of lead ore, during the 1880s and '90s. In the meantime, Y Fan mine near Llanidloes, in the words of David Bick, one of the leading authorities on the history of the metal mines of mid Wales, 'bequeathed its name to one of the most sensational mineral discoveries ever made in [the British Isles]'. It became the most productive lead mine in Britain, yielding about 4,300 tonnes of lead ore in 1870. In 1876, the mine's best year, Y Fan produced over 6,700 tonnes of lead ore and almost 2,000 tonnes of zinc ore. By the 1890s, however, the industry was in decline and even the high prices of lead and zinc during the First World War failed to revive it.

Nevertheless, remains abound. Besides the Silver Mountain Experience (formerly the Llywernog Silver-Lead Mine Museum and Caverns), near Ponterwyd, a visitor attraction which offers a less than satisfactory insight into the history of the industry in general and the old Llywernog mine in particular, the entire area is peppered with evocative relicts: ruinous buildings; scarred hillsides; barren spoil heaps; dressing floors; adits; shafts; leats; wheel-pits and tram-roads.

One such place is the site of the once mighty Cwmystwyth mine, an archaeological and geological resource of international significance situated a short distance upstream of Cwmystwyth village. Here, beneath Graig Fawr, the immense gashes of the most spectacular late eighteenth-century opencast workings in mid Wales were created by the rush of water (a technique known as hushing) deliberately released to scour the precipitous hillside and reveal the metalliferous veins. Alongside the river Ystwyth, the spoil heaps – the repository of waste rock and discarded minerals of no commercial value, together with occasional specimens of lead-grey galena (lead ore), lustrous brown sphalerite (zinc ore) and bright golden chalcopyrite (copper ore) that escaped the crushers – remain an attraction for inquisitive geologists and mineralogists alike. But that's not all. Also present is white milky quartz, a common but worthless component of the mineral veins, and a number of very rare minerals known only amongst knowledgeable mineralogists.

5. Mynydd Hiraethog to the Dee estuary

Silurian [443-417 million years ago –
Carboniferous [354-298 million years ago]

Oft prone to floods, nowhere is afon Conwy's impressive floodplain between Betws-y-coed and Dolgarrog narrower than 700 metres and broader than 1,000 metres. It is, in effect, the surface expression of a buried glacial trough, whose glacially-deepened rock floor in places is well over 100 metres below current sea level. The erosive power of the northward-flowing Conwy glacier, that occupied Dyffryn Conwy when the last glaciation was at its peak about 20,000 years ago, was greatly facilitated by the presence of the Conwy Valley Fault, a line of geological weakness that separates two highly contrasting territories.

To the west, the rocks underpinning the steep, craggy

1. The Conwy floodplain and gentle, west-facing valley-side slopes;
2. The craggy, wooded, east-facing slopes of the Conwy valley

Rocks of Wales

1. Mynydd Hiraethog; 2. Bryniau Clwyd

and well-wooded east-facing valley-side slopes that rise for the most part 200-250 metres above the floodplain, belong to the Llywelyn Volcanic Group, centered upon the great expanse of Y Carneddau, whose highest iconic summits – Carnedd Llywelyn (1,064 m) and Carnedd Dafydd (1,044 m) – rival that of Yr Wyddfa (1,085 m). The Llywelyn Group consists predominantly of resistant lavas and volcanic ashes (tuffs) and a lesser thickness of mudstones and siltstones, all of Ordovician age, whereas the far gentler, west-facing slopes of Dyffryn Conwy, cloaked with a patchwork of woods and pastures, are formed of softer, less resistant sedimentary rocks of Silurian age.

East of the Conwy valley lies Mynydd Hiraethog (sometimes known as the Denbigh Moors), an undulating upland plateau, much of it above 400 metres and whose highest summit, Mwdwl Eithin, is 532 metres above sea level. Once described by Walter Davies (better known as Gwallter Mechain; 1761–1849) as 'one of the most extensive and dreary wastes in the principality', the area's somewhat bleak and monotonous character, familiar to all who have driven along the A543 between Denbigh (Dinbych) and Pentrefoelas, is relieved by low summits, ill-drained river valleys, four small natural lakes, five reservoirs, extensive abandoned

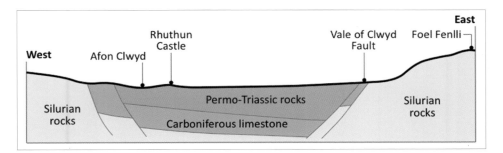

heather-clad grouse moors and vast coniferous plantations. Perhaps equally monotonous to the untrained eye is the geology, for the entire undulating tract of rolling hill country, between Dyffryn Conwy, in the west, and the western edge of Dyffryn Clwyd (Vale of Clwyd), in the east, is underlain by an alternation of sandstone, siltstone and mudstone, a succession of sedimentary rocks of Silurian age (443–417 million years old) swept into a marine basin by powerful westward- and northward-flowing ocean currents between 433 and 427 million years ago.

As striking as the junction between the Ordovician volcanic rocks and the Silurian sedimentary rocks in the Conwy valley is the sudden disappearance of the Silurian strata beneath the outcrop of the 350

million-year-old Carboniferous limestone along the western edge of Dyffryn Clwyd. Together with a few isolated outcrops of limestone, the sandstones, siltstones and mudstones of Silurian age make a dramatic reappearance along the eastern edge of the vale, where they form the foundation of Bryniau Clwyd (also known as Moelydd Clwyd [Clwydian Range]), designated an Area of Outstanding Natural Beauty.

Although the bedrock is largely hidden, the rocks forming the floor of the Vale of Clwyd, whose existance and character have been ascertained by sinking boreholes, are believed to be Triassic in age (251–195 million years old). If that proves to be correct, they rank as some of the youngest rocks of Wales, which in the

case of the vale are preserved on the floor of a rift valley, an elongate lowland bounded by faults: to the east an ancient fault line defines the western face of Bryniau Clwyd, a chain of summits extending from Prestatyn, in the north, to Llandegla, in the south; to the west, a complex succession of faults that greatly disturb the continuity of the outcrop of fossil-rich Carboniferous limestone – extensively utilized in the construction of the exterior wall of St Asaph Cathedral (Eglwys Gadeiriol Llanelwy) and the rock on which stands Denbigh and its castle dismantled in 1660 – delimit the eastern margin of the higher ground that rises towards Mynydd Hiraethog. Between Abergele and Rhuddlan, at the northern end of the vale, friable, red, hot-desert dune sandstones have been recorded, but further south in the neighbourhood of St Asaph, Denbigh and Rhuthun exposures of red sandstones are relatively scarce. However, blocks of red and yellow sandstone are particularly evident in the west wall and tower of St Asaph Cathedral,

whilst Rhuthun's medieval castle, originally called Castell Coch yn y Gwernfor (Red Castle in the Great Marsh), was constructed during the late thirteenth century atop a red sandstone ridge overlooking a strategic river crossing.

The Vale of Clwyd is, without doubt, one of the most clearly defined tracts of the Welsh landscape. Crowning the fault-line scarp of the Clwydian Range, 4 kilometres north-east of Rhuthun, is the summit of Foel Fenlli (511 m), an eminence second only in height to Foel/Moel Fama (554 m), the highest of the Clwydian hills upon which stands the remains of the Jubilee Tower, a monstrosity built in 1810–c.1812 to commemorate George III's fifty years as king. However, unlike Foel/Moel Fama, Foel Fenlli is topped by an Iron Age hill-fort and from its ramparts it is possible, on a clear day, to appreciate not only the splendour of the entire vale in a single panoramic view but also Hiraethog's upland plateau against the backdrop of Y Carneddau. Once memorably described by poet Gwilym R. Jones (1903–93) in his lyric poem entitled 'Dyffryn Clwyd' as *Eden werdd Prydain yw* (Britain's luxuriant Eden), today's agriculturally productive vale was, some 230,000 years ago, the

1. St Asaph Cathedral; © Gwasg Carreg Gwalch
2. Ffynnon Beuno and Cae Gwyn caves, Tremeirchion; 3. Pant y Pwll Dŵr limestone quarry

haunt of Neanderthal hunters, whose bones and those of their prey were found in Pontnewydd Cave, in the limestone cliffs above the floor of the Elwy valley, south-west of Llanelwy. Near the village of Tremeirchion, on the eastern side of the Vale of Clwyd, the limestone caves of Ffynnon Beuno and Cae Gwyn have yielded the stone tools of Early Palaeolithic hunter-gatherers, who occupied the site about 30,000–35,000 years ago, and the bones of animals such as woolly mammoth and woolly rhinocerous who roamed the vale during a period of cold climate immediately prior to the last glaciation, which was at its peak about 20,000 years ago.

East of the vale, the thirteen

1. *Triassic red sandstone*; 2. *Gateway to Rhuthun Castle*; 3. *A fossil coral, Carboniferous limestone*; 4. *Creigiau Eglwyseg escarpment*

prominent summits of the Clwydian Range – Moel Hiraddug (overlooking Dyserth), Moel Maenefa, Moel y Gaer, Moel y Parc, Penycloddiau, Moel Arthur, Moel Llys y Coed, Moel Fama, Moel Fenlli, Moel Eithinen, Moel Gyw, Moel Llanfair and Moel y Plas – overlook the outcrop of Carboniferous limestone, which in the vicinity of Llangollen forms the spectacular west-facing escarpment of Creigiau Eglwyseg. In addition to its influence on the area's topography, a substantial portion of the main Carboniferous limestone outcrop on and around Halkyn Mountain (Mynydd Helygain) to the south of Holywell (Treffynnon) was once not only the most important of the several former lead-mining districts of Wales, but also one of the largest and most important lead producers in Britain. Major exploitation occurred in the eighteenth and nineteenth century and when the last mine closed in 1987 it ended almost 2,000 years of mining, leaving in its wake a landscape scarred and pitted with shafts and spoil heaps. Although the metalliferous ores of lead and zinc concentrated along cracks

Fossil plants of the Brymbo Fossil Forest;
© Peter Appleton

(joints) and faults within the limestone are no longer exploited, the rock itself is excavated, for example, near the village of Rhes-y-cae. The aptly-named Pant y Pwll Dŵr (the water-filled hole) is an enormous, highly-mechanized quarry that annually produces huge quantities of stone and aggregates.

When traced eastwards towards the shores of the Dee estuary (Afon Dyfrdwy) between Talacre and Flint (Y Fflint), the Carboniferous limestone plunges beneath a cover of Coal Measures, some of which contain workable coal-seams. The coal itself is the legacy of luxuriant tropical swamps that flourished about 300 million years ago and formed part of an elongate forest-covered delta-plain that lay athwart the Equator and extended btween present-day Poland and the British Isles. The nature and character of such forests was dramatically brought to life following the discovery of the Brymbo Fossil Forest in 2003, during opencast mining operations on the site of the former Brymbo steelworks, which closed in 1990. Covering an area nearly half the size of a football pitch 7.5 kilometres north-west of Wrexham (Wrecsam), the site contains a fantastic variety of fossilized plants and trees within the rock succession consisting of coal, mudstone and sandstone. Designated a Site of Special Scientific Interest of international importance, its website features a collection of fascinating resources based on an exhibition entitled 'From Coal to Carnations: The Evolution of Plants'. Furthermore, plans are underway, led by the Brymbo Heritage Group, to establish an on-site, world-class visitor attraction and local learning centre.

Brymbo lies close to the northern boundary of the Denbighshire coalfield, traceable south as far as Chirk (Y Waun). Whereas all deep mining operations ceased following the closure of Bersham Colliery in 1986, a further ten years elapsed before the closure of Point of Ayr Colliery (Y Parlwr Du), the most successful coalmine in the Flintshire coalfield, traceable from Point of Ayr – the most north-easterly headland of mainland Wales – to Caergwrle in the south. When production came to an end in 1996 it was claimed that there were sufficient reserves, whose workings lay for the most part beneath the Dee estuary and the open sea, to last another century. The mine is remembered alongside the A548 at Ffynnongroyw, a former coalmining village, where part of the head-frame of one of the three deep shafts sunk between the 1860s and 1890s, was unveiled in 2015.

No less valuable than the coal are several of the Coal Measure sandstones that have yielded, over the centuries, useful building stones. St. Winefride's holy well (Ffynnon Santes Gwenfrewi) in Holywell, which has been a place of pilgrimage since the seventh century and claims to be the oldest visited pilgrimage site in Britain, is built of Gwespyr sandstone. Cefn y Fedw sandstone, on the other hand, was employed in the construction of Basingwerk Abbey (Dinas Basing), near Holywell, during the building of the early thirteenth-century seven-bay nave; St Cyngar's Church, Hope (Yr Hob), first mentioned in 1254; and Caergwrle Castle, dating from the late thirteenth century. The same stone was used to build Pont Cysyllte, Thomas Telford's magnificent aqueduct that carries the Llangollen Canal almost 39 metres above the waters of the Dee, near Froncysyllte. Completed in 1805, it was awarded World Heritage Site status in 2009.

1. Head-frame of Point of Ayr Colliery (Y Parlwr Du), Ffynnongroyw; 2. Pont Cysyllte aqueduct; © Gwasg Carreg Gwalch

6. Old Red Country: The Black Mountain and The Black Mountains

Devonian [417–354 million years ago]

Often likened in profile to a great wave 'petrified at the point of breaking', the steep north-facing escarpment carved entirely from Old Red Sandstone rocks – although many are neither red in colour nor sandstones – is traceable over a distance of about 55 kilometres, or somewhat longer if the proverbial crow were to deviate from the straight and narrow!

Along the crest of the wave is a string of over twenty-five summits well in excess of 609 metres (or 2,000 feet), forming an imposing wall of sandstone and mudstone divided into four distinct sections. The Black Mountain (Y Mynydd Du) in the west is separated from Fforest Fawr by a col at the head of Cwm Tawe, whilst a similar breach at the head of Cwm Taf Fawr is the dividing line between Fan

Fan Frynych escarpment

Fawr (734 m) – the eastern outpost of Fforest Fawr – and the summits of Corn Du (873 m) and Pen y Fan (886 m), the latter being the crowning glory of the Brecon Beacons (Bannau Brycheiniog). Beyond the lofty Beacons and the intervening Usk valley, lie the Black Mountains (Y Mynydd Du), an upland which shares the same Welsh name as its western counterpart and whose highest summit, Hay Bluff (Penybegwn; 677 m), coincidentally stands at exactly the same elevation as the highest point of Bannau Sir Gâr, at the western end of the Black Mountain!

Major trunk roads head through all three breaches, deepened and widened by the scouring action of 'ice age' glaciers escaping southwards, but the Romans, the premier road builders of yesteryear, made a beeline for higher glacially-sculptured cols. The road linking the Roman fort of Y Gaer, near Brecon (Aberhonddu) – built about AD 75 to accommodate a 500-strong cavalry unit originally recruited from Spain – and the coastal fort at Cardiff (Caerdydd) crossed the Beacons via Bwlch ar y Fan (599 m), a desolate col between

Fan y Big (719 m) and Cribyn (795 m). Further west, Sarn Helen, which connected the fort at Neath (Castell-nedd) with Y Gaer, headed through the heart of Fforest Fawr via a large col at a height of 446 metres, breaching the watershed between Fan Llia (632 m) and Fan Nedd (663 m), near the head of Cwm Senni.

Maen Madoc, a slender 2.7-metre-high column of red sandstone that stands alongside Sarn Helen, a short distance south-south-east of the col, is a poignant reminder that not all in the service of Rome who wearily trod such dreary, God-forsaken roads survived the ordeal, for sometime after AD 423, the year when the Roman occupation of Wales effectively came to an end, it was inscribed with the message that reads, in Latin: '[The stone] of Dervacus, son of Justus. He lies here'. North-east of the col, Sarn Helen traces a near straight line across the gently undulating plateau surface of Mynydd Illtud, skirting the two bogs of Traeth Bach

and Traeth Mawr, and site of the Mountain Centre – a National Park Visitor Centre. It boasts one of the most spectacular views of the majestic escarpment that forms not only the backbone of the Brecon Beacons National Park, designated in 1957, but also

1. Maen Llia, an impressive Bronze Age standing stone of Old Red Sandstone conglomerate, situated on the floor of the col between Fan Llia and Fan Nedd; 2. Traeth Mawr and the summits of Corn Du and Pen y Fan; 3. Llyn y Fan Fach; 4. Maen Madoc

the core of the Fforest Fawr Geopark, an area of outstanding geological heritage which, in 2005, became a member of the Global Network of Geoparks, as recognized by UNESCO.

That the glaciers of the Great Ice Age, which dawned about 2.6 million years ago and has yet to come to an end, were once hard at work is plain to see for Cwm Llwch, below the twin summits of Pen y Fan and Corn Du, is one of a quartet of symmetrical, parallel valleys along the scalloped scarp face that terminate in enormous ice-scooped amphitheatres. Similar striking glacial landforms are encountered east and west of the Beacons. Particularly noteworthy is the huge ice-carved hollow nestling at the foot of the precipitous north-facing cliffs of Bannau Sir Gâr and cradling the lovely Llyn y Fan Fach, the watery home of the beautiful Lady of the Lake. According to the well-known legend, she returned with her cattle, sheep, goats, pigs and horses to the inky depths of the lake after her husband, shepherd from the nearby farm of Blaen Sawdde, had inadvertently struck her '*tri ergyd diachos*' – 'three causeless blows' – with an iron object. No less impressive than the moraine-dammed Llyn y Fan Fach are the deep, ice-shorn and trough-shaped valleys of Fforest Fawr and the Black Mountains.

The partial glacial demolition of the mountains is pay-back time, for the 1,000-metre-thick, layered pile of Old Red Sandstone rocks of which they are composed are themselves the debris of the Caledonides, a mountain range of Himalayan proportions, uplifted during the rock-crunching collision between the two ancient continents of Laurentia and Avalonia, around 410 million years ago. Following the mayhem of continental collision, the newly-amalgamated continent lay within subtropical, desert latitudes, south of the Equator, and the Old Red Sandstone rocks of central south Wales, composed of strata attributable to late-Silurian and early Devonian times, were destined to accumulate along its south-eastern border.

But what tectonic forces had conspired to elevate, agents of erosion sought to destroy and as with any demolition process, massive quantities of debris were created. Under the influence of a semi-arid but seasonally wet subtropical climate, rain-swollen rivers carried with them huge quantities of sand, silt and mud – and occasionally masses of pebbles – that were deposited on the floor of wide river valleys and on extensive low-lying plains on the southern flanks of the rapidly eroding slopes of the Caledonian mountains. Whilst successive layers of sand were laid down by meandering and braided river systems, subject to periodic flash floods, the finer-grained particles of silt and clay were deposited layer upon layer on nearby floodplains and occasionally in seasonal floodplain lakes. Some of the finer material, however, may even have originated as dust, whipped up by ferocious winds that periodically swept across the lowlands.

But the deposition of debris, for the most part coloured deep red-brown due to the presence of a coating of hematite (ferric oxide) originating from the oxidation of detrital iron minerals under the scorching tropical Sun, was not continuous. In places, breaks in the deposition of sand, silt and mud led to the formation of nodular limestone soils – calcretes – typical of semi-arid areas. Known locally as 'cornstones', these fossil soils – formed when groundwater containing dissolved calcium carbonate moves upwards and evaporates – are generally found in the oldest Old Red Sandstone rocks of the area. Mostly mudstones that span the Silurian–Devonian boundary, such rocks outcrop along the scarp and lower slopes of the Black Mountains that tower above the Wye valley (dyffryn Gwy), and occupy all but the higher scarp slopes of the Brecon Beacons–Fforest Fawr–Black Mountain escarpment, south of the Usk valley (dyffryn Wysg) between Brecon and Trecastle (Trecastell).

Distinct on account of their grey-green rather than red colour, the 300 metre-thick pile of the overlying Senni Beds are famous, for they are locally rich in plant fossils. Although the earliest land plants made their first appearance in mid-Silurian times, the sandstones of the Senni Beds, speckled with glistening flakes of white mica, have been described as 'one of the most important horizons in the world for Lower Devonian plants', dating from around 410 million years ago. But these primitive colonizers are unlike anything found today. For example, the simple branching, leafless and blackened stems of *Cooksonia*, no more than 10 centimetres tall, flourished together with other primitive land plant on the banks of

streams and around pools, providing tiny oases of green in what was otherwise a barren landscape, devoid of vegetation.

But rivers and freshwater lakes also provided a habitat for other forms of life.

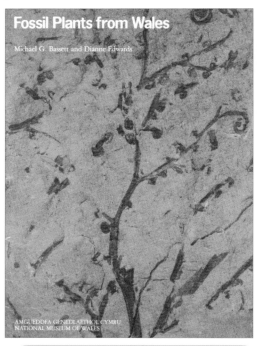

Fossil Plants from Wales

Michael G. Bassett and Dianne Edwards

AMGUEDDFA GENEDLAETHOL CYMRU
NATIONAL MUSEUM OF WALES

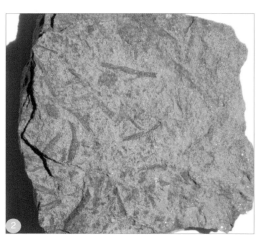

1. *Roadside (A470) quarry at the foot of Craig y Fro: a source of the Senni Beds;*
2. *Fossil plants from the Senni Beds*

The fossilized whole and dismembered remains of the primitive, jawless, armoured fish that lived in some of the rivers and lakes have also been found in the Senni Beds. So, too, have ripple marks, formed by the flow of water over loose sand, and the irregular polygonal outlines of desiccation cracks, produced as layers of fine-grained silt or mud were baked and dried under the blistering heat of the Sun and later infilled.

Resting upon the Senni Beds, bands of red-brown and purple-brown micaceous sandstones, separated from one another by layers of mudstone, reign supreme. Known as the Brownstones, they form the sheer rock walls that rise above Llyn y Fan Fach and Llyn y Fan Fawr in the west, and the 200-metre-high cliffs below the two iconic, flat-topped summits of the Brecon Beacons. However, in order to discover why Pen y Fan and Corn Du wear small flat caps, a strenuous walk up one of several well-trodden paths that lead to both summits is unavoidable. The path that heads southwards through Cwm Llwch is by far the most dramatic route. But before tackling its steepest section, there's no better place to pause for breath than on the shores of Llyn Cwm-llwch, a classic, text-book example of a lake dammed by glacial deposits. It occupies the floor of a small, natural amphitheatr or cirque, nestling beneath the shadow of the cold, north-east-facing cliffs of Craig Cwm-llwch, themselves the walls of a larger valley-head cirque, the source of the Cwm Llwch glacier during the height of the last 'ice age', some 20,000 years ago. The hugely impressive mounds of glacial deposits – known as moraine – accumulated around the snout of the small glacier that occupied the hollow during a brief cold period at the very end of the last 'ice age', between 13,000 and 11,500 years ago.

Viewed from the lake, which formed following the glacier's final disappearance 11,500 years ago, the ribs of harder sandstone in the cliffs at the head of Cwm Llwch appear horizontal. However, each layer is, in fact, tilted gently southwards, a dip that was imposed on the entire stack of Old Red Sandstone rocks during a period of powerful earth movements that climaxed at the end of Carboniferous times, around 300 million years ago, and known as the Variscan Orogeny. Tumbling streams within the gullies that scar the escarpment face cascade over the

Rocks of Wales

sandstone steps, whilst the intervening layers of mudstone beyond the gully margins are, in places, adorned with arctic-alpine plants at or very near their southernmost limit in Britain. Whilst the lime-deficient sandstones are unacceptable to many alpines, the mudstones are sufficiently limy to support colourful drapes of purple saxifrage (*Saxifraga oppositifolia*) that flowers at Easter time.

From the shores of the nine-metre deep Llyn Cwm-llwch, whose floor was once said to lie at a depth far in excess of the combined length of the bell ropes of Llan-faes church in Brecon, the path zig-zags up the backwall of the cirque, before climbing steadily upwards along the lip of Craig Cwm-llwch to the top of Corn Du. A short, steep section of path, a mere stone's throw from the summit, marks the outcrop of the aptly-named Plateau Beds of late Devonian age, a sequence of harder and more resistant pebbly sandstones that cap Corn Du and nearby Pen y Fan. Here, there's no perceptible break to be seen between the topmost bed of the Brownstones and the lowermost layer of

the Plateau Beds, but over in the west it's possible to see that the tilt of the Plateau Beds capping Bannau Sir Gâr is somewhat less than that of the underlying Brownstones. Though now hard to comprehend, the change in tilt represents a break in excess of 10 million years, during which time the Brownstones were subject to erosion before the Plateau Beds were deposited.

So, the two small caps atop the highest summits of the Brecon Beacons are remnants of a once extensive sheet of relatively hard, pebbly sandstones deposited on top of the eroded Brownstones. Look beneath your feet and here too you will see ripple-marks – fossilized sand waves whose steeper slopes point in the direction of river flow. Sadly, however, they have suffered irreversible damage under the tramp of 350,000-odd walkers who annually make it to the top, most of whom are content to ignore the denuded rocks at their feet at the expense of the awe-inspiring views from the two highest vantage points of Wales south of the rugged grandeur of Aran Fawddwy–Aran Benllyn and Cadair Idris, almost 100 kilometres to the north.

South of Pen y Fan, in the disused

1. *The Brownstones exposed in the cliffs below Corn Du and Pen y Fan;*
2. *Llyn Cwm Llwch*

Abercriban quarry on the eastern slopes of Cwm Taf Fechan and near the southern end of the Pontsticill reservoir, the Plateau Beds themselves are topped by the very youngest Old Red Sandstone rocks of the area. Deposited by braided rivers about 360 million years ago, and probably spanning the Devonian-Carboniferous boundary, the grey-white sandstones were used in the construction of the reservoir, as facings for the rubble-filled dam wall. In fact, Pontsticill reservoir is one of four in Cwm Taf Fechan – a rain-soaked area experiencing an annual total in excess of 2400 millimetres – and one of a total of twelve located, for the most part, in the glacial trough-like valleys south of the main Old Red Sandstone escarpment. Almost all of these man-made ribbon lakes were established not only to provide a much-needed regular supply of clean drinking water for the urban population of the south Wales coalfield, but also to satisfy the insatiable demands of now defunct heavy industries.

1. *The Plateau Beds capping Corn Du;*
2. *The severely eroded summit of Corn Du;*
3. *Llyn Dôl-y-gaer and the snow-covered summits of Pen y Fan (right) and Corn Du (centre)*

First to be constructed in Cwm Taf Fechan in 1858, was the Pentwyn reservoir, the dam wall being located at Dôl-y-gaer, where the valley is conspicuously narrow. For the inhabitants of Merthyr Tudful and Dowlais, eager to escape, albeit for just a day, the grime, smoke, stench and noise of their wretched daily lives, the creation of Llyn Dôl-y-gaer, as it came to be known locally, proved to be an unrivalled attraction. During the 1860s, crowds in excess of 10,000, that had travelled northwards on foot, in carriages or by rail, would attend the annual July regattas and congregate on the grassy slopes beside the lake to enjoy the fresh air, 'the lovely mountainous scenery' and the festivities – all to the accompaniment of the Cyfarthfa Brass Band, established by Robert Thompson Crawshay (1817–79), master of Cyfarthfa Castle and owner of the Cyfarthfa ironworks.

But all was not well, for the incompetent engineer responsible for selecting the site of the dam wall did not appreciate the geological significance of the narrow bottleneck of the valley. Astride Cwm Taf Fechan at Dôl-y-gaer sits a truly gargantuan block of Carboniferous limestone, bounded by faults and set in the midst of the Brownstones. Narrow, gorge-like valleys, such as the rocky, pothole-strewn Pont-sarn gorge through which the Taf Fechan flows a short distance south of Pontsticill, are typical of Carboniferous limestone country, and so too are caves and subterranean drainage networks. The fissured and fractured bedrock foundations of the dam proved its undoing. The limestone leaked like a sieve. All attempts to plug the leakages, that exceeded 50 million litres of water a day in the early years of the twentieth century, failed dismally. Because the stability of the dam wall itself was in question, it was decided in 1911, that a new dam should be built downstream, on the less permeable and fault-free mudstones and sandstones of the Brownstones. To this day, the six kilometre-long Pontsticill–Pentwyn reservoir, completed in 1927, is a monument to a spectacular example of an engineering disaster.

The fault-lines crossing Cwm Taf Fechan are part and parcel of the so-called Neath Disturbance, a complex zone of ancient fractures and crumpled strata, reawakened and reactivated during the Variscan Orogeny. From Neath, near the shores of Swansea Bay (Bae Abertawe), the course of the rupture can be traced north-eastwards as far as Hereford, a distance of almost 100 kilometres. As far as Pontneddfechan, about 18 kilometres north-east of Neath, the Vale of Neath (Cwm Nedd) is as straight as a ramrod, the valley having been excavated along the broken bedrock hidden below its floor. But for some 20 kilometres beyond the village the most obvious expression of the Disturbance is the severely disrupted outcrop of the Carboniferous limestone, together with 'islands' of the same grey rock left stranded amidst a 'sea' of Old Red sandstones and mudstones in the vicinity of Dôl-y-gaer.

But despite its antiquity, the Neath Disturbance is still a seismic hot-spot. At 9:45 on the morning of Wednesday, 27 June 1906, an earthquake, whose epicentre lay in the Swansea area, caused 'profound and widespread alarm' the length and breadth of southern Wales, whilst its 'terrible vibrations' damaged property in nearby towns and villages alike, as its terrifying but short-lived shock waves rippled through the rocks. History was repeating itself and not for the first time. Swansea, near the southern end of the zone of upheaval that slices through the

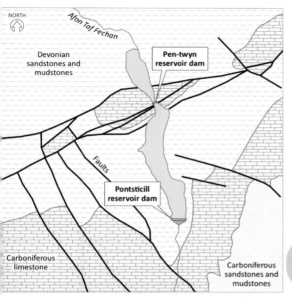

Carboniferous limestone exposed alongside the Brecon Mountain Railway at Dôl-y-gaer Overleaf: Pontsticill Reservoir

south Wales coalfield and the Old Red Sandstone rocks, south of the great escarpment, had been rocked on four previous occasions: in 1727, 1775, 1832 and 1868. Given their periodicity, the British Geological Survey had ventured to suggest some time ago that a further earthquake in the area was probably due in the near future. And so it transpired. At about 2:30 pm on Saturday, 17 February 2018, residents the length and breadth of Wales, south-west England and the Midlands experienced the tremors of a 4.4 magnitude quake whose epicentre lay near the village of Cwmllynfell, about 15 kilometres north of Neath. Caused by the sudden fracturing and movement of rock at a depth of 7.4 kilometres below the surface, the earthquake was the largest to be recorded on mainland Britain in almost 10 years.

7. The Valleys and the South Wales Coalfield

Carboniferous [354–298 million years ago]

Built by Gilbert de Clare, one of Henry III's most powerful and ambitious barons, an air of massive menace still pervades Caerphilly (Caerffili) Castle. Its purpose was to prevent lowland south Wales from falling into the hands of Llywelyn ap Gruffudd, Prince of Wales, who controlled most of mid- and north Wales. Although Llywelyn successfully attacked the fortress on two occasions between 1268 and 1271, it was finally completed during the 1270s. Gilbert's castle, records John Newman, author of *The Buildings of Wales: Glamorgan* (1995), was 'probably the earliest large-scale use of a stone which later became Glamorgan's commonest building material'. Indeed, no other stone typifies

1. *Caerffili Castle;* © Gwasg Carreg Gwalch
2. *Cyfarthfa Castle;* 3. *Terraced housing built of Pennant sandstone, Rhondda valley*

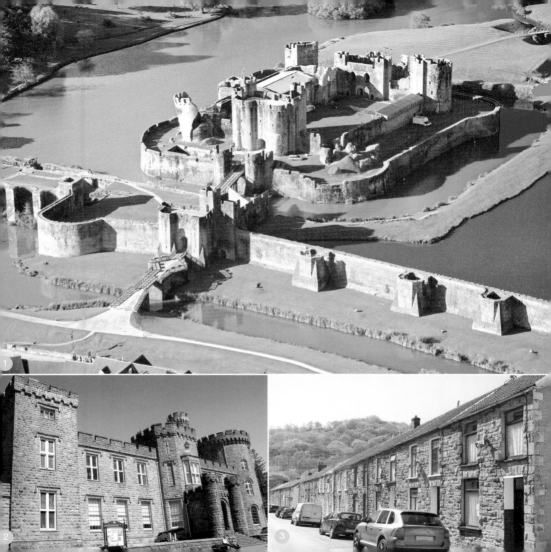

1. *Rhondda Heritage Park, established on the site of the Lewis Merthyr Colliery, whose pit-head buildings were constructed of Pennant block-stone; 2. Craig yr Hesg Quarry*

the south Wales valleys more than the bluish-grey Pennant sandstone that weathers to a rusty-brown colour when exposed to the elements. Over 550 years after the completion of Gilbert's mighty fortress the selfsame stone was used in the construction of Cyfarthfa Castle, the grand castellated mansion built in 1824–5 by Robert Lugar, a prominent London architect and engineer, for William Crawshay, the great ironmaster, at the staggering cost of £30,000 (well in excess of £2,000,000 in today's money!). Described as 'the most impressive monument of the Industrial Iron Age in south Wales', the mansion was sited to overlook the family's ironworks in Merthyr Tudful, the largest works of its kind in the world during the first and second decades of the nineteenth century. But, prompted by the sinking of dozens of deep coalmines and an explosive growth in population, it was during the second half of the nineteenth century and the early decades of the twentieth century that the quarrying of Pennant sandstone reached its zenith.

Between 1850 and 1914 the population of the Rhondda valley, the most celebrated of all the Valleys, increased from a mere 2,000 souls to well over 154,000. Demand for housing was all but insatiable and venturesome and enterprising builders and quarry owners had a field day. In the Rhondda valley alone, 16,000 homes were built between 1881 and 1914. The once tree-lined Valleys – shorthand for, from east to west, the Llwyd, Ebbw Fach (Ebwy Fach), Ebbw Fawr (Ebwy Fawr), Sirhowy (Sirhowi), Rhymney (Rhymni), Bargod Rhymni, Bargod Taf, Taff (Taf), Cynon, Rhondda Fach, Rhondda Fawr, Ogwr Fach, Ogwr Fawr, Garw, Llynfi and Afan valleys – were transformed for the most part into long lines of contour-hugging terraces in one gigantic entrepreneurial leap. Besides workers' houses, shops and pubs, chapels and churches, Miners' Halls and Workmens' Institutes, and pit-head buildings built of Pennant block-stone, pavements too were universally constructed of Pennant flagstones, dug from quarries large and small that still scar the higher valley-side slopes. One of the largest quarries, Craig yr Hesg, near Pontypridd, is still in operation and in 1930 it supplied stone for the construction of the splendid memorial commemorating none other than Evan James, author of 'Hen Wlad fy Nhadau', the Welsh National

Anthem, and his son, James James, who composed the music. Standing in Ynysangharad Park in the centre of Pontypridd and set against the backdrop of Mynydd Craig-yr-hesg, the memorial, designed and executed by Sir William Goscombe John RA, the acclaimed Cardiff-born sculptor, consists of two bronze figures, the one representing music and the other poetry 'mounted on pedestals of blue pennant stone'.

The imprint of Pennant sandstone is as evident in the form of the landscape as it is on the area's built heritage. It's this resistant sedimentary rock, incorporating thin bands of mudstone and thin seams of coal, which is the foundation of the uninhabited high moorland plateau that rises almost imperceptibly when traced northwards across the width of the great east–west elongate basin that is the south Wales coalfield, which in its entirety can be traced westwards as far as the shores of St Bride's Bay (Bae Sain Ffraid) in Pembrokeshire. From Taff's Well (Ffynnon Taf), north-west of Cardiff (Caerdydd), it's possible to follow the Ridgeway Walk path (Ffordd y Bryniau) either west to the summit of Garth Hill (Mynydd y Garth; 307 metres) or east to the top of Craig yr Allt (273 metres), that stand astride the Taff valley. Both hill masses mark not only the southernmost extension of the bleak high plateau but also part of the steep, south-facing escarpment of the Pennant sandstone, whose layers are inclined steeply northwards.

At Craig y Llyn, beyond the upper reaches of Cwm Rhondda Fawr, the gently-undulating high plateau has climbed almost imperceptibly to an altitude of about 600 metres. It terminates at the edge of a spectacular north-facing escarpment that towers high above the forlorn winding gear and associated buildings of Tower Colliery, the last deep mine in south Wales that finally closed in January 2008 after all workable coal-seams had been exhausted. Below the lip of the escarpment lies Llyn Fawr, that occupies one of several huge rock-bound amphitheatres scooped out by 'ice age' glaciers. Although the horseshoe-shaped backwall of the cirque is largely masked by scree, ribs of Pennant sandstone, gently-inclined towards the south, are evident in the dark cliffs high above the lake shore, into which votive offerings were thrown over 2,500 years ago. Fortuitously, the Iron Age hoard, which included two massive

1. The monument commemorating Evan and James James, composers of the Welsh National Anthem; 2. Craig y Llyn; 3. The high summits of the Old Red Sandstone escarpment, north of Craig y Llyn

bronze cauldrons, bronze axes and sickles and a finely-decorated iron sword, was discovered in the lake-bed peat during the conversion of the originally smaller Llyn Fawr into a reservoir, during the early years of the twentieth century.

From the vantage point above the lake a magnificent panorama beckons, for the eye is immediately drawn northwards towards the high summits of the Black

Mountain, Fforest Fawr and Brecon Beacons that form the greater part of the north-facing Old Red Sandstone escarpment. To the south, the southerly-dipping layers of red sandstones and mudstones are overlain by Carboniferous limestone, which in turn is overspread by 'Millstone Grit', whose outcrop marks the northern rim of the south Wales coalfield and its Coal Measures, the coal-bearing rocks that occupy the low ground beyond the foot of Craig y Llyn. In common with the Old Red Sandstone, Carboniferous limestone and 'Millstone Grit', the Coal Measures – or more precisely the Lower and Middle Coal Measures – also dip gently in a southerly direction and are capped and hidden for the most part beneath a cover of Pennant sandstone of Upper Coal Measure age. Indeed, because the Coal Measures forming the northern rim of the saucer-shaped coalfield basin are inclined at a much gentler angle than those of the southern rim, they outcrop over a broad area at the northern end of the Cynon, Taff, Rhymney, Sirhowy, Ebbw Fawr, Ebbw Fach and Llwyd valleys. Here, readily accessible coal-seams and ironstones, worked in levels at no great depth, were two of the essential raw materials that spawned a string of early ironworks along the northern margin of the coalfield during the late eighteenth century. Foremost were those at Merthyr, Dowlais and particularly Blaenavon (Blaenafon), now a World Heritage Site that serves as a microcosm of the formative years of the Industrial Revolution.

In contrast to the northern tract, large-scale exploitation of the rich coal-seams within the central coalfield had to await the sinking of deep pits along the floors of deeply entrenched valleys that rivers, aided and abetted by the unrelenting grinding action of 'ice age' glaciers, had cut down through the thick pile of Pennant sandstone that forms the high plateau. Between 1864 and the turn of the century, twenty-five deep pits were sunk along the floor of Cwm Rhondda Fawr alone, a valley famously and unforgettably described by the collier-poet Thomas Evans (better known by his bardic name, Telynog), who earned his bread and butter in a pit near Aberdare (Aberdâr) during the 1850s, as being '*culach na cham ceiliog*' (narrower than a cockerel's stride)! And in one of the pits near Tonpentre, 'the celebrated Four Foot Seam', was encountered, a coal much vaunted by the Ocean Coal Company of

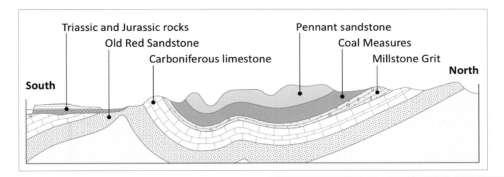

South

Triassic and Jurassic rocks
Old Red Sandstone
Carboniferous limestone

Pennant sandstone
Coal Measures
Millstone Grit

North

Cross-section of the south Wales coalfield

Cardiff 'for Steam Navigation and Railway purposes'. Whereas the Rhondda was noted for steam-coal production, pits in the eastern and south-eastern section of the coalfield, such as Big Pit, Blaenafon, sunk in 1860, yielded bituminous coal, used in the making of gas and coke as well as for domestic purposes. Designated Big Pit National Coal Museum – National Museum of Wales – in 2001, it's the only remaining colliery site in the Valleys that offers visitors the chance to descend 90 metres to the pit floor in order to explore working conditions underground and examine what was once a working coalface.

But coal, the fuel of the industrial age, makes up only a tiny proportion (probably less than 2%) of the total thickness (about 2,500 metres) of the Lower and Middle Coal Measures. Nowhere is its insignificance more apparent than at sites such as Ffos-y-frân, currently the United Kingdom's largest opencast coalmine situated on the outskirts of Merthyr. The overriding impression is that the Lower and Middle Coal Measures here and elsewhere are largely made up of vast thicknesses of dark mudstones, siltstones and occasional layers of sandstone, but scarcely coal. But such a comparison does give a very misleading impression of the relative time-span represented by a coal-seam, on the one hand, and layers of mudstone and siltstone, on the other. Whereas the peat needed to generate a metre of coal could

OCEAN (Merthyr) STEAM COAL

PROPRIETORS

THE OCEAN COAL COMPANY, LTD.,

11, BUTE CRESCENT, CARDIFF.

Output : 9,500 TONS PER DAY.

This Coal is unrivalled for Steam Navigation and Railway purposes.
It is well known in all the Markets of the world for
ECONOMY IN CONSUMPTION, ITS PURITY AND DURABILITY.

It is largely and in many cases exclusively used by the PRINCIPAL STEAM
NAVIGATION COMPANIES at Home and Abroad.

OCEAN (MERTHYR) STEAM COAL

solely was used by the Cunard Company Steamers " **Mauretania** " & " **Lusitania** "
in creating a Record for the most rapid Atlantic Passages.

THE OCEAN COMPANY supply the requirements of the English Admiralty
for trial trips, for the use of the Royal Yachts, and other special purposes.

The Ocean Coal Company, Limited, have the largest unworked area of the celebrated
Four Feet Seam of Coal in South Wales.

take anything up to 7,000 years to accumulate, far fewer years would have been required for the deposition of the same thickness of mud and silt on vast delta-plains, on or near the Equator, sweltering under a wet, tropical climate.

For most of the time the delta-plains, dissected by large meandering and braided rivers, were covered by dense, luxuriant swamp forests. But periodically, the southerly-flowing rivers, draining a landmass situated over what is now mid-Wales, would burst their banks, drowning and killing the steamy, rain-soaked forests, before finally sealing the wood and other plant material under thick layers of mud and silt. The sea, too, would occasionally inundate the coastal plains and leave behind thin tell-tale layers of sediment – marine bands – containing the remains of marine creatures. But as the floodwaters subsided, swamp forest vegetation would once again colonize the land and flourish until the next devastating flood. As the same cycle of events was repeated time and time again, the heat and compression imposed by deep burial of the subsiding

mass of deposits would trigger the slow conversion of each peat layer into coal.

Towards the end of Carboniferous times, some 300 million years ago, convergence of two ancient supercontinents – Gondwana and Laurussia – triggered the Variscan Orogeny, a period of powerful earth movements and mountain building, which signalled the end of Lower and Middle Coal Measure times. As a result of the changed geographical and topo-graphical circumstances, huge quantities of river-deposited sand, swept northwards by rivers draining the rising Variscan mountains to the south, buried the richly-fossiliferous Lower and Middle Coal Measures under what would become Pennant sandstone, a rock largely devoid of any signs of life.

In contrast, the swamps and raised river banks – levees – of Lower and Middle Coal Measure times had sustained life in a profusion never before seen on land. The waterlogged freshwater swamps and marshes not only provided the ideal environment for the growth of giant club mosses, tree ferns and horsetails, but also conditions much to the liking of molluscs, similar to present-day freshwater mussels. Insects also flourished: colossal dragonfly-

1. Big Pit National Coal Museum, Blaenafon; 2. Ffos-y-frân opencast coalmine
© Miller Argent (South Wales)

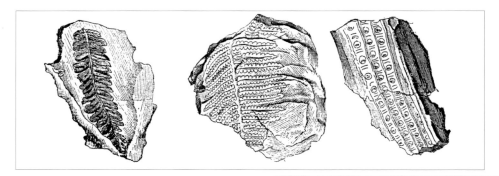

Sketches of the fossil plants that Edward Llwyd acquired on visiting a coalmine near Neath

like creatures; cockroaches; spiders and giant millipedes. The marine bands, on the other hand, traceable the length and breadth of the south Wales coalfield, yield coiled ammonite-type fossils, called goniatites. Each band represents a particular moment in time when the sea inundated the land, a sea-level rise triggered by changes in the extent of a vast south polar ice sheet, which during late Carboniferous times covered present-day South Africa, southern India, southern Australia and Antarctica, land masses all gathered together as part of the ancient supercontinent of Gondwana.

But it was fossil plants, rather than the far less common remains of sea creatures to be found in elusive marine bands, that attracted the attention of early fossil collectors, and none more so than Edward Llwyd (Lhuyd), the curator of the Ashmolean Museum at Oxford. Coal Measure plants, or *Lithophyta*, as he called them, fascinated and intrigued Llwyd and whilst on his visit to Wales in 1693 the talented and proud Welshman was clearly delighted to discover that 'The Coalpits of Glamorganshire, affoard as much variety of subterraneous plants as those of Gloc. [Gloucestershire] & Somersetsh[ire].' Fine illustrations of three of the different species that he collected on his visit to a coalmine near Neath (Castell-nedd) are included amongst his contributions to Edward Gibson's revised edition of

EDVARDI LUIDII

A P U D

Oxonienſes Cimeliarchæ Aſhmoleani

LITHOPHYLACII BRITANNICI

ICHNOGRAPHIA.

S I V E

Lapidum aliorumque Foſſilium Britannico-
rum ſingulari figura inſignium; quotquot ha-
ctenus vel ipſe invenit vel ab amicis accepit,

DISTRIBUTIO CLASSICA:

Scrinii ſui lapidarii Repertorium cum locis
ſingulorum natalibus exhibens.

Additis rariorum aliquot figuris ære inciſis; cum
Epiſtolis ad Clariſſimos Viros de quibuſdam circa ma-
rina Foſſilia & Stirpes minerales præſertim notandis.

Nuſquam magìs erramus quàm in falſis inductioni-
bus: ſæpe enim ex aliquot exemplis Univerſale
quiddam colligimus; idque perperàm, cum ad
ea quæ excipi poſſunt, animum non attendimus.
Du Hamel.

L O N D I N I:

Ex Officina M. C. cIɔ Iɔc xcix.

William Camden's *Britannia*, published in
1695. Not surprisingly, Llwyd devoted one
entire section of his *Lithophylacii Britannici
Ichnographia* (1699), the first ever
catalogue of British fossils, to *Lithophyta*,
most of the specimens illustrated having

been collected in Wales.

But the most avid and passionate
collector of fossil plants was David Davies
who in 1883, at the tender age of twelve,
started work in Penrhiw-ceibr Colliery in
the Cynon valley. By his twenty-first
birthday, the self-taught Davies had not
only been appointed colliery manager, but
had also been bitten by the fossil-
collecting bug, a fate which quickly earned
him the endearing title of Dafydd Ffosil
(David of the fossils)! Davies spent his
most important and scientifically
productive years at Gilfach Goch, near the
head of Cwm Ogwr Fach, where fossils
became the focus of his life. It was here
that the irrepressible young man began to
collect fossil plants, in addition to some
animal fossils, in a much bigger and more
systematic way. Davies' unique collection
of fossil plants of the south Wales coal
basin, amassed prior to his untimely death
in 1931, amounts to an astonishing 16,000
specimens or so, housed in the National
Museum of Wales, Cardiff. It's a reference
collection of inestimable value since the
mines that yielded the fossils have long
since closed and are no longer accessible.

Gone too are the prodigious coal tips
which once mantled valley sides and hill

In search of Fossil Plants:
the life and work of
David Davies
(Gilfach Goch)

Barry A. Thomas

AMGUEDDFA GENEDLAETHOL CYMRU
NATIONAL MUSEUM OF WALES

claiming the lives of 144 people, including 116 schoolchildren. But despite tip clearance, slope instability is endemic and widespread in the Valleys, and most large and small landslides are located at or near spring-lines at the junction of the porous Pennant sandstone and the underlying impervious mudstones of the Lower and Middle Coal Measures. Even so, most landslides have been and still are triggered by the effects of injudicious human actions and enterprises on the glacially overdeepened flanks of the valleys that cut across the coalfield with scant regard for the underlying bedrock geology.

The headwaters of the Sirhowy, Rhymney and especially the Taff rise well north of the coalfield proper and as they flow towards the south-south-east they not only cut across the entire width of the major east–west trending asymmetric downfold – syncline – of the coal basin, but also large and small subsidiary folds and some of the faults within its bounds. Although the remaining rivers have their sources within the coalfield, they too cut across folds and faults and breach the southern rim of the main syncline, a structure formed by intense northward-directed pressure during the Variscan

tops in their hundreds, and were for many years the happy hunting grounds of young and old fossil hunters alike. Their wholesale clearance or 'landscaping' was finally prompted by the catastrophic collapse on the morning of 21 October 1966 of Tip Number 7 of Merthyr Vale Colliery, a 34-metre-high black pyramid of spoil and one of seven sited menacingly on the steep valley-side slopes above the village of Aber-fan, near Merthyr. The deadly tongue of saturated spoil, which accelerated down-slope, engulfed the local junior school and eighteen houses,

Orogeny as the southern continent of Gondwana ploughed headlong into the northern continent of Laurussia. A drainage pattern so spectacularly discordant to the main syncline of the south Wales coalfield, let alone other lesser Variscan folds and faults, could only have developed after the rivers had first established their near parallel courses on the surface of younger rocks blanketing the underlying Carboniferous strata and gently inclined towards the south-south-east. Were the rivers first established on a blanket of Cretaceous chalk, as has been suggested by some? Maybe. Or did they originate on a lowland surface uplifted and tilted during the Alpine Orogeny, about 25 million years ago, as others would claim? Perhaps. The nature and age of the surface on which the original drainage pattern was developed and later superimposed on the underlying Carboniferous rocks is still hotly debated, but once the rivers were established, the coalfield was ultimately laid bare and the Valleys born.

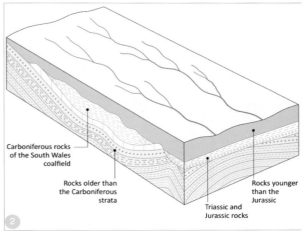

Carboniferous rocks of the South Wales coalfield

Rocks older than the Carboniferous strata

Triassic and Jurassic rocks

Rocks younger than the Jurassic

1. The Pen-twyn landslide, Ebwy valley;
2. A diagram depicting the coalfield's original drainage pattern?

8. Rocks astride the Milford Haven Waterway

Devonian [417–354 million years ago] – Carboniferous [354–298 million years ago]

Holyhead
ANGLESEY
Bangor
Bethesda
Caernarfon
1
LLŶN PENINSULA
SNOWDONIA
Bardsey Island
Harlech
3
Trawsfynydd
Dolgellau
Barmouth
CADAIR IDRIS
Prestatyn
Abergele
Holywell
St Asaph
Flint
Denbigh
Betws-y-coed
5
Rhuthun
Pentrefoelas
Wrexham
Llangollen

Cardigan Bay
Aberdyfi
Y Borth
PUMLUMON
Aberystwyth
New Quay
Cardigan
Llanidloes
Rhayader
4

2
PRESELY HILLS
St David's Head
St David's
St Bride's Bay
Skomer Island
Skokholm Island
St Ann's Head
Freshwater West
Tenby
Manorbier
8
Swansea
Brecon
BLACK MOUNTAINS
BLACK MOUNTAIN
BRECON BEACONS
6
Neath
Aberdare
Merthyr Tudful
Blaenafon
7
Pontypridd
Caerphilly
Bridgend
Cardiff
Ogmore-by-sea
Penarth
9
Barry Island

miles 20
kilometres 40
Contains Ordnance Survey data
© Crown copyright and database right 2018

The coastal village of Penally (Penalun), south-west of Tenby (Dinbych-y-pysgod), lies at the eastern end of an ancient Bronze Age trackway called The Ridgeway. This old path follows part of a narrow but prominent ridge of high ground which is traceable west-north-west, over a distance of about 26 kilometres as the crow flies, as far as the headland north of West Angle Bay, at the mouth of the Milford Haven waterway (dyfrffordd Aber-daugleddau). Between Penally and Lamphey (Llandyfái), the Ridgeway proper – now the course of a minor road that undulates along the ridge crest – is at its highest at Norchard Beacon (108 m), an excellent vantage point from which to begin to appreciate the full significance of the long narrow hilltop.

The ridge marks not only

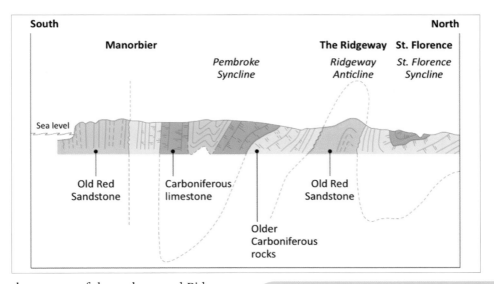

South   North

Manorbier   The Ridgeway   St. Florence

Pembroke Syncline   *Ridgeway Anticline*   *St. Florence Syncline*

Sea level

Old Red Sandstone

Carboniferous limestone

Old Red Sandstone

Older Carboniferous rocks

Cross-section of the pattern of folded rocks between St Florence and Manorbier

the outcrop of the aptly-named Ridgeway Conglomerate, a relatively hard and resistant rock band composed of a sequence of 415-million-year-old Devonian conglomerates, sandstones and mudstones, but also an upfold – the Ridgeway Anticline – flanked for the most part by blue-grey Carboniferous limestone and younger rocks of Carboniferous age occupying complementary downfolds: the St Florence Syncline to the north and the Pembroke Syncline to the south. The older Devonian rocks are, more often than not, reddish in colour, and hence have long been called the Old Red Sandstone.

Located on the lower ground to the north of Norchard Beacon is the attractive ancient village of St Florence, whose parish church, with its tall tapering tower, is built of Carboniferous limestone. To the south lies the village of Manorbier (Maenorbŷr) which, like St Florence, is also situated on Carboniferous limestone, the rock utilized to build the imposing grey walls of 'the castle called Maenor Pyrr

[Maenorbŷr], that is, the mansion of Pyrrus'. But although constructed of limestone, the castle, first mentioned in 1146, is actually set dramatically upon a rocky spur of Old Red Sandstone, whose rocks plunge steeply northwards beneath the Carboniferous limestone forming the southern limb of the Pembroke Syncline.

From the beach at the head of Manorbier Bay (Bae Maenorbŷr), the castle is reminiscent of the great Crusader castles of Syria, and it was within its walls that Gerald de Barri, part Norman, part Welsh, spent his happy boyhood days. His love of his birthplace is unquestionable, for in later life Gerald, who liked to be known as Giraldus Cambrensis (Gerald of Wales [Gerallt Gymro]) in order to mark himself out as a champion of Welsh separateness, was unashamedly of the opinion that 'in all the broad lands of Wales Manorbier is the most pleasant by far'.

Without doubt, the coastal scenery does go some way towards substantiating Gerald's bold claim. From the bay which 'looks out towards the Irish Sea', it's well worth walking south along a section of the Wales Coast Path towards the rocky headland of Priest's Nose, but pausing for a while besides the King's Quoit, a fairly

unobtrusive Neolithic burial chamber or cromlech, with spectacular views overlooking Manorbier Bay and the wave-cut rock platform extending westwards as far as East Moor Cliff. The rocks hereabouts, whose upended layers are as neat as a pack of cards stood on end, are predominantly thick red mudstones,

1. St Florentius' Church, St Florence; 2. Manorbier Castle; 3. King's Quoit

which were quarried in order to construct the cromlech consisting of a 10 tonne capstone, supported originally by three small side-stones, one of which has collapsed. A closer look reveals that the megaliths contain innumerable pale-coloured knobbly lumps of limestone, nodules which form in soils in hot, semi-arid regions as groundwaters evaporate after rain, precipitating clots of lime in the process. Such fossil soils, called calcretes, are typical of the floodplains of ephemeral, seasonal rivers or lakes in dry, desert regions and hence they provide an insight into the various environments in which the huge quantities of mud, silt and sand that make up the Old Red Sandstone of south Wales were deposited.

But it's not only calcretes that are found amongst the layers of mudstone, siltstone and sandstone (some of which are actually green in colour) along the wave-battered cliffs between the Priest's Nose and Old Castle Head, site of a Ministry of Defence firing range. On numerous occasions during early Old Red

1. Freshwater West beach; 2. Great Furzenip as seen from Little Furzenip;
3. The conglomerate at the boundary between the Silurian and Devonian rocks

Sandstone times, violent volcanic eruptions, not too far distant, blasted billowing clouds of volcanic ash high into the atmosphere that subsequently rained down, blanketing large areas under layers of fine-grained ash. Three of the layers of compacted ash (tuff) present are between one and 3.5 metres thick; substantially thicker than the thickest ash layers deposited in a 95-kilometre-long swathe downwind of Mount St Helens, in Washington State, USA, following upon the volcano's cataclysmic eruption on 18 May 1980. Those layers were only 5 to 13 centimetres thick. However, the tuffs of south Pembrokeshire record volcanic activity about 415 million years ago, triggered by the progressive convergence of the two ancient continents of Gondwana and Laurussia. Some also contain fossils, or at least the foraging tracks, burrows and faecal pellets of anonymous creatures.

There's no better place to gain a closer look at the type of rocks forming the cliffs between the Priest's Nose and Old Castle Head than Freshwater West, one of the wildest beaches in Pembrokeshire, much frequented by surfers but dangerous for swimmers, due to the presence of powerful rip currents. Hereabouts, the Old Red Sandstone strata between the headlands of Little Furzenip and Great Furzenip, south of the magnificent sandy beach, are inclined steeply towards the south. Indeed, were it not for the fact that the area south of Little Furzenip lies within the boundary of the Castlemartin artillery range, a walk towards Great Furzenip would involve traversing progressively younger layers of rock.

On the foreshore below the car park and toilets alongside the B4319, the layers of conglomerate forming a series of small rocky outcrops mark the approximate boundary between Silurian rocks to the north and Devonian strata to the south. Above the conglomerate, containing abundant angular fragments of quartz, the succeeding c.415 million-year-old Old Red Sandstone rocks are composed mainly of red and green mudstones, although a short distance north of Little Furzenip, lies the 2.8-metre-thick, yellow-weathering Townsend Tuff, one of the most conspicuous of all the tuff bands to be seen in a number of localities north and south of the Milford Haven waterway. The sediments forming the rocks were deposited by ephemeral streams in a hot,

semi-arid environment, whilst the thick red mudstones in particular contain clear evidence of soil formation, for they are full of pale grey limestone nodules and tubes (tubules), typical of calcretes.

To the south of Little Furzenip, the sequence of red and green mudstones and sandstones and occasional layers of conglomerate, deposited by meandering rivers flowing across an extensive alluvial plain stretching from present-day Pembrokeshire into the Welsh Borderlands, also contain calcretes. Though apparently barren, the sun-scorched landscape was not entirely devoid of life, for some of the layers of river-lain sandstones contain the remains of early land plants, the plates and scales of strange, primitive, armoured fish, and burrows and tracks of anonymous arthropods.

The Ridgeway Conglomerate, the foundation of the conspicuous ridge of high ground between Penally and West Angle, actually outcrops in the face of the low cliffs between Little Furzenip and Great Furzenip, but somewhat surprisingly it makes no impression whatsoever on the topography thereabouts.

Though impossible because of the presence of the Castlemartin artillery

range, a walk south from Freshwater West beach to the bold Carboniferous limestone headland of Linney Head, via Little Furzenip and Great Furzenip, would have involved a journey of about 57 million years through geological time; a journey from the Silurian–Devonian boundary to the Devonian–Carboniferous boundary. Environmentally the recorded changes were nothing if not dramatic. The retreat of Silurian seas heralded the formation of the semi-arid Old Red Sandstone landmass, which itself was ultimately inundated by a warm, shallow, tropical sea in early Carboniferous times, about 350 million years ago.

To experience a walk back through geological time one need only visit nearby West Angle Bay, eroded along the axis of a small syncline and bounded by beds of Carboniferous limestone that plunge beneath the sandy beach. By following the Wales Coast Path towards the north-west, the rocks beneath one's feet record the gradual transition from shallow water, lime-rich marine sediments (the Carboniferous limestone) to land-based alluvial-plain sediments (the Ridgeway Conglomerate), that outcrop on the headland overlooking the Milford Haven waterway. The latter is a superb example of a ria formed by the drowning of the lower reaches of the river Cleddau and its tributaries by the post-glacial rise in sea level.

Though dominated by red mudstones and sandstones, there are significant differences between the sequence of Old Red Sandstone rocks north and south of the Milford Haven waterway, a harbour proclaimed by none other than Horatio Nelson to be one of the finest he had ever seen. But strictly speaking, the dividing line between the rocks north and south of the haven, is not the waterway but rather the Ritec Fault, a deep-seated fracture which formed the boundary between two different areas of deposition. From the coastal marshes between Tenby and Penally, once the site of a tidal estuary, the trace of this major fracture heads west-north-west along the line of the Ritec valley and then onwards before striking the haven shoreline between Pembroke Dock and the mouth of the Pembroke river. Thereafter, the hidden fault-line's presumed path follows the central axis of the waterway, making a beeline for Dale, a

popular sailing centre on the north shore of the haven. The fractured and shattered rocks within the fault zone not only determined the course of the lowermost reach of the river Cleddau, but also the line of the anomalous valley which links Dale and West Dale Bay.

Excavated by a torrent of glacial meltwater during the last 'ice age', the 'channel' that mirrors the course of the fault-weakened rocks effectively isolates the Dale peninsula from the adjoining mainland. The last recorded movement along the Ritec Fault may well have occurred as recently as August 1892 when the shock waves generated by an earthquake, with its epicentre near Pembroke, were strong enough to cause some local damage to houses and rattle buildings throughout south-west Wales, Devon and Cornwall. But, in reality, it's an ancient fracture, a fault-line that was probably most active during a period of powerful earth movements and mountain building – the Caledonian Orogeny – which climaxed about 410 million years ago.

The Old Red Sandstone rocks north of the Ritec Fault are the product of torrential but seasonal southward-flowing rivers that swept enormous quantities of mud, silt and sand, together with lesser amounts of coarser debris, off the rapidly eroding Caledonian mountains to the north. The resulting mudstones, siltstones and sandstones are magnificently exposed in the warm, red-coloured cliffs fringing the narrow inlet of St Bride's Haven, in the bounding headlands of the beautiful Marloes Sands, and between Sandy Haven and the town of Milford Haven. And like the rocks south of the fault, they too incorporate fossil soils (calcretes) and layers of volcanic ash, including the conspicuous and extensive Townsend Tuff, named after a locality near the village of Dale.

But the Ridgeway Conglomerate and the so-called Skrinkle Sandstones overlying the conglomerate, which are encountered south of the haven are nowhere to be found north of the waterway. North of the Ritec Fault they are replaced by the Cosheston Beds, a thick sequence of grey-green river-deposited sandstones, siltstones and conglomerates. Well-exposed at Mill Bay on the shores of the Daugleddau, north of the village of Cosheston, the grey-green sandstones were once thought to be the source of the Altar Stone, the largest of all the 'foreign stones' found at Stonehenge. Sadly, for those who wished to claim a Pembrokeshire connection for the stone slab, detailed research has shown that it was actually derived from the Old Red Sandstone Senni Beds, 'somewhere between Kidwelly [Cydweli] and Abergavenny [Y Fenni]', far to the east of Milford Haven and the Presely Hills (Y Preselau), source of most but not all of the so-called 'bluestones' that form the inner circle and inner horseshoe of Stonehenge.

Furthermore, it's now known that the source of most of the 'bluestones' – mainly a collection of boulders and pillars of 470-million-year old 'spotted' dolerite, once thought to have been derived from the craggy, south-facing summit of Carn Meini overlooking the dispersed hamlet of Mynachlog-ddu – was Carn Goedog, a tor on the northern slopes of the Presely Hills. Moreover, it seems that 'most archaeologists are fairly sceptical now about the likelihood of ocean-going bluestones'. Instead, they were supposedly dragged overland – over hill and dale, rivers and marshes – via an imaginary route all the way to the site of Stonehenge with the aid of an improbable superhuman labour force of 'thousands'. In truth, however, only the vast ice sheet, which

1. West Angle Bay; 2. The Dale–West Dale Bay meltwater channel; 3. St Bride's Haven; 4. Carn Goedog; 5. Cobbler's Hole

covered the whole of Wales and the greater part of Britain about 450,000 years ago, would have been capable of transporting such a load of glacial erratics from the Presely Hills to the western fringes of Salisbury Plain.

The outcrop of the grey-green sandstones of Mill Bay lies astride the axis of another major upfold – the Burton Anticline – which can be traced west-north-west from the village of Carew to beyond Rosemarket, north of Neyland. Like all the west-north-west–east-south-east trending upfolds of varying widths and amplitudes to the south of the Ritec Fault, the Burton Anticline was also once one of a series of parallel mountain ridges elevated during the Variscan Orogeny, a major and prolonged episode of mountain building that climaxed in late Carboniferous times, about 300 million years ago.

But, despite the scale and intensity of folding, the corrugations imposed upon both the Old Red Sandstone and Carboniferous rocks of varying hardness, caught in the grip of the colliding continents, have counted for little in landscape terms, for the entire area has subsequently been pared-down and reduced to what is, in places, a snooker-table-flat plateau surface. On a small-scale, the discordant relationship between the crumpled rocks and the coastal plateau is

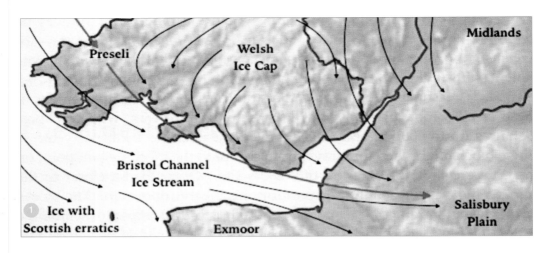

beautifully illustrated at St Ann's Head, which guards the approach to the Milford Haven waterway. A mere stone's throw from the old coastguard station and lighthouse set atop the flat-topped headland is Cobbler's Hole, where the red rocks – splendidly displayed in the walls of the steep-sided inlet – have been compressed into a small but mightily impressive syncline and complementary anticline. To appreciate the incongruous relationship on a broader scale, head four kilometres north-north-west to a point where the Coast Path hugs the Red Cliff at the southern end of Marloes Sands. Viewed from here, the 40–50 metre-high coastal plateau that truncates the southerly-dipping Old Red Sandstone rocks of Skokholm Island and nearby Gateholm appears as flat as a pancake. Even more dramatic is the 40–50-metre-high surface planed with spectacular indifference across the intensely folded Carboniferous limestone strata that underlies the territory occupied by the Castlemartin tank range. The proximity of such surfaces to present-day intertidal rock platforms suggests that these coastal plateaux are also remnants of wave-cut platforms, fashioned by the sea perhaps no more than about five million years ago.

But despite the planation, the imprint of folds and faults has not been entirely eradicated. South of the Milford Haven waterway, many of the streams mirror the trend of the west-north-west–east-south-east fold axes. So, too, does the orientation of the magnificent 10 kilometre stretch of Carboniferous limestone cliffs between Linney Head and St Govan's Head, which have been cut into a fantastic variety of forms, whilst the highly-indented six kilometre-section of Old Red Sandstone cliffs between Freshwater East and Old Castle Head, has been eroded along innumerable faults. And Manorbier Bay is no exception, whose geologically-controlled configuration proved irksome to Manorbier's most famous son. 'If only the rocky headland to the south bent round northwards a little further', wrote a frustrated Gerald in his journal, *The Journey through Wales*, 'it would make a harbour most convenient for shipping.' Evidently, geology, coupled with the coast's exposure to the full force of fierce Atlantic gales, has been the bay's salvation!

1. *Paterns of ice movement;* © Brian John
2. *Gateholm Island*

9. The Vale of Glamorgan

Triassic [251–195 million years old] – Jurassic [195–251 million years old]

Wales, though endowed with a plentiful supply of workable building stone of various colours and textures, is not noted for material with a consistency and texture fine enough to admit of being cut 'freely' in any direction with the aid of a toothed saw and skilfully carved with a mallet and chisel. Whilst the county of Glamorgan – one of the thirteen historic counties of Wales – is also largely lacking in highly-prized 'freestone' the same cannot be said of the Vale of Glamorgan (Bro Morgannwg), lying for the most part south of the M4 motorway linking Cardiff (Caerdydd) and Bridgend (Pen-y-bont ar Ogwr). Edward Williams, alias the celebrated Iolo Morganwg (1747–1826),

1. Iolo Morganwg (*an engraving by Robert Cruikshank*); 2. Sutton stone arrow slit, Ogmore Castle; 3. Site of former Sutton stone quarry

who in his first handbill, dated 1779, advertised himself as a marble-mason specializing in 'all sorts of chimney-pieces, monuments, tombs, [and] headstones', knew all too well that 'freestone of various and excellent sorts may be dug in many places' in his native Vale of Glamorgan. Poet, visionary and antiquary of renown, Iolo was a scholar of genius who took an active interest in an incredibly wide range of subjects. Not the least of his interests was geology, and he undoubtedly possessed a detailed and unrivalled knowledge of workable block stone in Glamorgan. Always at pains to extol the virtues of his beloved native county, Iolo was adamant that Sutton stone, in particular, quarried 'near the mouth of Ogmore river' was not only 'a limestone equal in texture to the Portland' – an exceptionally fine quality freestone famously used for public buildings in Wales and the length and breadth of Britain – but also 'superior to it in whiteness and durability'.

1. *Interior of Ewenni priory church;* © *Gwasg Carreg Gwalch* 2. *The arcaded parapet of Swansea Castle, fashioned from Sutton stone; 3. Sutton stone overlying Carboniferous limestone, near the southern end of Ogmore beach*

On this occasion, the veracity of Iolo's somewhat exaggerated claim is, to say the least, questionable. But Sutton stone, once dug from a series of small quarries strung along the hillside above the village of Ogmore-by-sea (Aberogwr), on the western shores of the Vale of Glamorgan, was a highly-prized freestone widely-used the length and breadth of south Wales. Easily recognized on account of its whitish-grey colour, coarse-grained texture and pitted appearance, Sutton stone dressings are plainly to be seen in the walls of the twelfth-century Ogmore Castle (Castell Aberogwr), that stands on the banks of the Ewenni river, a little over two kilometres north-east of the old quarries. About three kilometres upstream of the ruined castle, Sutton stone ashlar and dressings dominate the interior of the beautiful twelfth-century priory church at Ewenni, dedicated to St Michael, 'the most complete and impressive Norman ecclesiastical building in Glamorgan', according to John Newman, author of *The Buildings of Wales: Glamorgan* (1995). West of its source area, imported blocks of the distinctive freestone were dressed and incorporated in buildings such as Neath Abbey (Abaty Nedd), Swansea Castle

(Castell Abertawe), Kidwelly Castle (Castell Cydweli) and St Dogmael's Abbey (Abaty Llandudoch), on the banks of the Teifi estuary, in north Pembrokeshire. To the east, Sutton stone, tough and resistant to weathering, was extensively used in the first rebuilding of Llandaff Cathedral (Eglwys Gadeiriol Llandaf) during the early twelfth century, and in the subsequent century was transported a considerable distance inland, where carved blocks were employed to dress Caerphilly Castle (Castell Caerffili), a masterpiece of military architecture.

So overgrown and indistinct are almost all the old quarries where quarrymen once laboured to dislodge the tough pale rock with the aid of levers and wedges, the only good exposure of Sutton stone now lies at the far end of a level, two-kilometre-long footpath that heads southwards from the beach-front car park at Ogmore as far as the coastal cliffs near the foot of a steep, dry valley. If you stand on the highest rock-cut platform above the sea, the rock beneath your feet is 350-million-year old Carboniferous limestone. Take a closer look and you will see that its upper surface bears signs of smoothed and sculpted surf-scoured hollows and shallow channels typical of tidal erosion. Turn your back on the sea and you're confronted by Sutton stone, one of the youngest hard rocks to be found in Wales, deposited on top of the wavy, wave-eroded surface of Carboniferous limestone at the beginning of the Jurassic period, about 200 million years ago. Here, the boundary between the two rock-types represents a mind-boggling 150-million-year gap in Earth history!

Contrary to its horizontal appearance, the Sutton stone, which is largely devoid of any signs of bedding, is in fact banked up against the cliffs of one of several islands of Carboniferous limestone that, for a time, stood above the so-called Tethys Ocean, before its level rose and submerged the extensive desert plains and rocky limestone hills that characterized the preceding Triassic period. Some of the angular limestone fragments, dislodged from the wave-battered cliffs now concealed within the hillside, were transformed into pebbles, others to limy mud by the incessant pounding surf, before being thoroughly mixed with the fragmented shells of marine creatures and finally cemented together by the deposition of calcareous material dissolved in the warm sea water. The end result was Sutton stone, a pebbly limestone deposited close to island shorelines, early in the Jurassic period when, what is now the Vale of Glamorgan, lay about 30°–40° north of the Equator.

In the deeper but still relatively shallow water beyond the archipelago of islands, the Sutton stone and overlying thinly-bedded limestones pass both laterally and vertically into the distinctive ribbed alternations of hard, blue-grey limestones, often less than 30 centimetres thick, and softer, thin, grey mudstones of the Blue Lias. It's these rocks that give rise to the spectacular cliffs of the Vale's Jurassic coast between Dunraven (Dwnrhefn) and Barry Island (Ynys y Barri), and again between Swanbridge and Lavernock (Larnog), to the south of Penarth. Unbroken except where rivers and streams debouch into the sea, the vertical cliffs between Dunraven and Breaksea Point (Aberthaw [Aberddawan]) form the greater part of the Glamorgan Heritage Coast, designated in the 1970s in order to conserve the dramatic coastal scenery and unique character of a cliff-line which provides one of the best exposures of the Blue Lias anywhere in Britain.

Having accumulated layer by layer on the sea floor, the 150-metre-thick pile of Blue Lias is famous for its beautifully preserved fossils. They include large and small ammonites and bivalved shells, corals, crinoids, wood and plant material swept into the shallow sea from nearby land, and, in places, rare fossil vertebrae and other remains of streamlined marine reptiles known as ichthyosaurs, who feasted, amongst other things, on unsuspecting ammonites. At low tide, a stroll along St Mary's Well Bay, west of Lavernock Point (Trwyn Larnog), can be especially rewarding, for numerous flattened, spiral shells of one particular ammonite, called *Psiloceras*, are to be seen on the surface of some of the layers of mudstone. And that's not all. You will find that other rock layers, that form part of the broad wave-cut platform at the foot of the cliffs, are covered with fossil 'oyster' shells called *Gryphaea*. It is also widely-known as the Devil's Toenail and its thick, strongly curved, ribbed shell make it one of the most easily recognized fossils in Britain.

In fact, *Gryphaea*, which is also found in the rocks exposed on Dunraven beach, was once claimed to be 'the most famous of the Glamorgan fossils'. But today that honour surely belongs to *Dracoraptor hanigani*, a small, slim, meat-eating dinosaur, about 70 centimetres tall and 200 centimetres long, whose skeletal remains were discovered by the brothers Nick and Rob Hanigan during a fossil-hunting expedition near Lavernock Point in spring 2014. This Welsh dinosaur (*Dracoraptor* means 'dragon robber', *Draco* meaning 'dragon', the emblem of Wales, whilst its specific name, *hanigani*, honours its finders) lived at the very beginning of the Jurassic period, about 200 million years ago, 'possibly making it the oldest Jurassic dinosaur in the world', according to members of staff of National Museum Wales: Cardiff (Amgueddfa Genedlaethol Cymru: Caerdydd), where the amazing fossil now resides. Wales can also claim one of the earliest dinosaur footprint sites in Europe. Discovered in April 1974 and preserved in layers of red and buff-coloured sandstone and mudstone exposed on the seashore east of Barry Island and about six kilometres west of Lavernock Point, the footprints date back to the middle of Triassic times, about 215 million years ago.

The layered Blue Lias rocks exposed in the cliffs of St Mary's Well Bay are in the form of a broad, gentle downfold or syncline. In contrast, the rocks in the cliffs north of the bold headland of Nash Point (Yr As Fach), near Marcroes, are bent into a broad, upfold or anticline. Numerous faults too slice through the rocks, disrupting the continuity of layers either side of such breaks along which intermittent movement has taken place. A short distance north of the car park at the head of Dunraven Bay, fracture zones in the cliff face and rocks exposed on the foreshore are picked out not only by shattered bedrock but also irregular veins of calcite infilling cracks and gashes that developed along the fault lines. Being easy pickings under the lash of storm waves, such lines of weakness are often the site of repeated rock falls, in addition to gullies traceable across wave-cut platforms. So conspicuous is one such gully that dissects the wave-cut platform about 400 metres south of Nash Point that it has earned the name of Gwter Fawr (the great gully). Not that faults, such as those at Dunraven, are wholly to blame for the instability of the

1. Blue Lias cliffs, Dunraven; 2. A large ammonite lying beside the Heritage Coast Centre, Dunraven; 3. Eroded shells of Gryphaea; 4. Dracoraptor hanigani

© Artwork by Bob Nichols (palaeocreations.com)

Bendrick Rock; footprint of a three-toed dinosaur

Trwyn y Witsh (misspelt Witch on the Ordnance Survey 1:25,000 map), a 63-metre-high windswept headland on the south side of the bay. *En route* the path heads past what little remains of the site of the nineteenth-century Gothic mansion of Dunraven Castle (Castell Dwn-rhefn), demolished in 1962, which lay within the ramparts of an Iron Age hill-fort. Unlike the cliff-top hill-fort atop Nash Point, which has been largely destroyed by coastal erosion during the last 2,000 years, Dunraven fort has suffered less damage, because here the Blue Lias rests upon a firmer foundation of Carboniferous limestone outcropping at the foot of Trwyn y Witsh. But, despite its resistance, the explosive force of storm waves have taken their toll. Wave attack, directed at the base of the headland and subsequent cliff collapse has not only eaten into the fort on both sides, but has also hastened the retreat of the cliffs south of the headland and added significantly to the width of the wave-cut platform at their base. From a vantage point high above the shore, the view south towards Cwm Nash (Cwm yr As Fawr) is truly breathtaking, particularly at low tide, for ahead of the majestic 50–60-metre-high cliffs between

cliffs. Within the rocks, sets of natural cracks – joints – at right-angles to one another have also been exploited by the sea, giving rise to enticing but unstable sea caves, which are a striking feature of the coastal scenery near Tresilian Bay, east of St Donat's (Sain Dunwyd).

For those wishing to know more about the coastal scenery, its well worth visiting the Glamorgan Heritage Coast Centre, situated about 200 metres up-valley of Dunraven Bay car park, before climbing the grassy path that leads to the top of

Trwyn y Witsh and Cwm Bach the 300-metre-wide, near horizontal shore platform takes on the appearance of a geological map. The swirling and, in places, recurved and disrupted outcrops of the harder layers of limestone mirror the pattern of small but intricate folds and faults within the cliffs. Though inconsequential in scale and geometry when compared to the enormous structures produced by the unimaginably powerful tectonic forces that gave rise to the Alps, about 25 million years ago, the folds within the Blue Lias, are the ripple effects of those Alpine earth movements, set in motion as the African and European continents crashed headlong into one another, a collision that obliterated all but the last vestiges of the Tethys Ocean. And minor though the dislocations may be, the faults are the permanent scars of quakes that accompanied the continental collision.

Although natural outcrops of the Blue Lias are few and far between away from the coast, the rock has left an indelible stamp on the Vale's landscape, a fact not lost on Iolo Morganwg, who spent much

1. Cliffs of Blue Lias between Trwyn y Witsh and Cwm Nash; 2. Ruined walls of Dunraven Castle

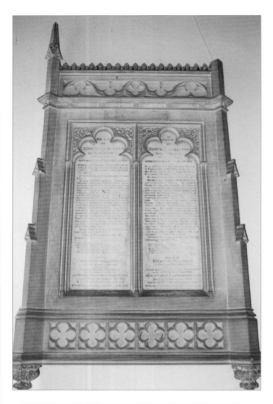

Flemingston Church: large double tablet, with inscriptions in Welsh and English 'In memory of Edward Williams (Iolo Morganwg) of this village, stonemason, bard and antiquary'

of his life at Flemingston (Trefflemin) and is remembered in the village church. Most of the quarries, he observed, yielded 'stone for lime of the most excellent quality' and 'stone not only for common rough walling but such as may be hewn into very neat ashlar at moderate expense', ashlar which was in his somewhat biased opinion 'much more beautiful', than either Portland stone or Bath stone! In reality, it will not cut to a smooth surface, but because it's intersected by numerous vertical joints, the layers of blue-grey limestone could be readily quarried and its value as a building material was recognized as soon as stone buildings began to be erected. The Romans used Blue Lias in the walls of their fortress at Cardiff, whilst the Normans made extensive use of the stone for the walling of their castles in the Vale. It was also used from time to time by the stonemasons who built Llandaff Cathedral.

Furthermore, much of the Vale's appeal – an area of quiet beauty – can be attributed to the buildings constructed largely, if not exclusively, of Lias limestone quarried in the immediate locality. Nestling for the most part in secluded valleys below the level of the coastal plateau – itself, in all probability, the dissected remnants of an ancient wave-cut platform – the villages and their squat, square-towered churches are attractively built of the local limestone. Very much off the beaten track, the tiny, loose-knit village of Llancarfan, where St Cadog's Church probably stands on the site of a monastic community established by Cadog during the fifth or sixth century, is a gem. So too is the small town of Llantwit Major (Llanilltud Fawr), where the parish church preserves the memory of the important monastic church, which by tradition was founded by St Illtud, possibly as early as the year 500. Not surprisingly, Llantwit (*twit* being a contraction of an Irish form of Illtud's name) fascinated Iolo the stonemason and historian, who avidly collected information about its traditions and buildings, in addition to the natural features, agriculture and, of course, geology of the town and parish.

Llantwit Major Parish Church

10. Cardigan Bay and Cantre'r Gwaelod

(*The Devensian Glaciation [at its maximum c.20,000 years ago] – the present-day*)

Stand on the foreshore at Aberdyfi on a quiet summer's evening, listen intently and you may hear the barely audible, muffled chimes of bells, wafted ashore by a gentle onshore breeze. Immortalized by the eighteenth-century folk song 'Clychau Aberdyfi' (The Bells of Aberdyfi), legend has it that they are the bells of the sixteen fair cities of Cantre'r Gwaelod (The Lowland Hundred), the lost kingdom of Gwyddno Garanhir, drowned beneath the waters of Cardigan Bay (Bae Ceredigion), a story first documented in *Llyfr Du Caerfyrddin* (The Black Book of Carmarthen), a thirteenth-century Welsh manuscript that contains the earliest written collection of Welsh poetry. It's a tragic tale and

1. *The Dyfi estuary and Aberdyfi;*
2. *Newgale Sands: the peat that sustained the 'forest grove'*

1. *John Wesley;* 2. *Newport Bay*

according to the familiar nineteenth-century version of events, the demise of Cantre'r Gwaelod was all due to the negligence of Seithennin, keeper of the embankments and floodgates built to protect the populous and fertile plain from the ravages of the waves. During a night of feasting, Seithennin over-imbibed and in his drunken stupor he forgot to close the floodgates. On that fateful stormy night the sea burst through the embankments, flooding the greater part of Gwyddno'r realm.

But tantalizing wave-torn strips of Cantre'r Gwaelod survived the catastrophe. In 1188, Gerald of Wales (Gerallt Gymro) and Archbishop Baldwin embarked upon a preaching and recruiting tour to gain support in Wales for the Third Crusade. Whilst crossing Newgale Sands (Traeth Niwgwl), on the shores of St Bride's Bay (Bae Sain Ffraid), several miles south of Cardigan Bay, Gerald recalls that a few years prior to his visit, following a storm of 'unprecedented violence' that had denuded the shore of sand, 'the sea shore took on the appearance of a forest grove', the tree trunks of which 'shone like ebony'.

Some 400 years later on the very same beach, George Owen, author of *The Description of Penbrockshire* (1603), also witnessed 'an infinite number of butts of trees in the places where they had been growing', a sure sign 'that the sea in that place has intruded upon the land'. And in his notes included in Edmund Gibson's revised edition of William Camden's *Britannia* (1695), Edward Llwyd (Lhuyd), the acclaimed naturalist, linguist, antiquarian and keeper of the Ashmolean Museum, Oxford, stated that he too had observed, at low tide, tree stumps and roots along the beach between Y Borth and Aberdyfi. But it was the itinerant Methodist preacher, John Wesley, on one of his frequent visits to Wales, who was the first to begin to appreciate the extent of the inundation. On discovering tree roots, leaves and nuts in a layer of peat on the shores of Newport Bay (Bae Trefdraeth), south-west of Cardigan (Aberteifi), in July 1777, he concluded that not only had the whole bay been dry land 'a few centuries ago', but that 'formerly it was dry land from Aberystwyth to St David's Point [Penmaendewi]'. In fact, on the basis of the evidence described by Wesley and later writers, it's clear that the whole of Cardigan Bay, now the haunt of porpoises and dolphins, was once dry land, for eroded remnants of submerged forests have been recorded at a number of locations between Llanaber, north of Barmouth (Y Bermo), and Aber-mawr, west of Fishguard (Abergwaun).

Although rarely visible, the submerged forest on the beach at Clarach, north of Aberystwyth, tells us that between about 7,000–6,500 years ago this small portion of Cantre'r Gwaelod supported a woodland composed of pine and birch, which was later supplanted by alder, hazel and oak, prior to its destruction by saline water as sea level rose. The submerged forests between Y Borth and Ynys-las, best exposed following the removal of sand between high- and low-water mark by the action of winter storms, tells a similar story. The trees at Ynys-las, along with 300-year-old oaks embedded in peat further south, died about 6,000 years ago.

Besides the submerged forest beds, tradition has it that a series of enigmatic offshore ridges, only partially exposed to view at very low tides, also bear testimony to the inundation of Cantre'r Gwaelod. Robert Vaughan (*c.*1592–1667), the seventeenth-century antiquary of Hengwrt,

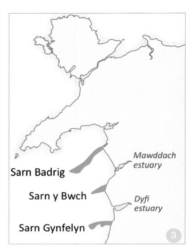

1. *Ynys-las submerged forest*; 2. *A pebble of Ailsa Craig microgranite*; 3. *The three* sarnau; 4. *The landward end of Sarn Gynfelyn;* © David Evans

Sarn Badrig

Sarn y Bwch

Sarn Gynfelyn

Mawddach estuary

Dyfi estuary

near Dolgellau, admired for having secured by far the best collection of historic Welsh manuscripts amassed by one person, was convinced that the ridge of boulders, cobbles and gravel called Sarn Badrig, traceable south-westwards over a distance of *c.*24 kilometres from the coast at Ynys Mochras, south of Harlech, was at one time 'a great stone wall, made as a fence against the sea'. Sarn y Bwch, situated midway between Barmouth and Aberdyfi, extends *c.*6 kilometres offshore, whilst Sarn Gynfelyn, north of Aberystwyth, is approximately 13 kilometres long. Although William Owen Pughe, joint editor of *The Myfyrian Archaiology of Wales* (1801–07) and antiquary noted for his gullibility, boldly claimed to have identified the remains of Caer Gwyddno (Gwyddno's fort) at the seaward extremity of Sarn Gynfelyn, all three of the supposed man-made *sarnau* (causeways) are natural phenomena.

Clues to their likely formation lie partly in the fact that the ridges are located seaward of the southern margins of the Glaslyn–Dwyryd, Mawddach and Dyfi valleys, along which large glaciers flowed westwards during the last 'ice age'. At the peak of the so-called Devensian Glaciation about 20,000 years ago, mainland Wales – except for south Pembrokeshire, south Gower and the Vale of Glamorgan – was buried beneath a large ice cap centred over the Arennig mountains, east of Trawsfynydd. At that time, the magnificent panoramic backdrop of the mountains of Eryri (Snowdonia), currently enjoyed by all crossing Traeth Mawr via William Madocks' (1773–1828) Cob at Porthmadog, would have been hidden from view by the combined mass of the Glaslyn–Dwyryd glacier relentlessly ploughing its way towards Tremadog Bay (Bae Tremadog). There, its accumulated load of ice-scoured rock fragments of all shapes and sizes and pulverized rock debris, concentrated in the sole of the glacier and along its margins, was unceremoniously dumped as the ice began to melt and retreat, some 17,000 years ago. The boulder-clay cliffs at Ynys Mochras, at the landward end of the morainic ridge of Sarn Badrig, are full of so-called glacial erratics; chunks of rock in the form of boulders and cobbles of a bewildering variety of rock-types – some ice-scratched – derived largely from sources which today lie within the catchment area of the rivers Glaslyn and Dwyryd. Largely but not exclusively, for

some boulders of igneous rock at the south-western end of Sarn Badrig are known to have come from the vicinity of Arennig Fawr, transported westwards by ice which overtopped the Rhinogydd, the rugged line of summits between the Dwyryd and Mawddach estuaries.

In similar fashion to the Glaslyn–Dwyryd glacier, the westerly-flowing Mawddach glacier plastered thick accumulations of glacial deposits not only along the valley floor but also the coastline beween Llwyngwril and Tonfannau, south of the now spectacular Mawddach estuary. And at Tonfannau the load of morainic debris heads offshore in the form of Sarn y Bwch. Sarn Gynfelyn, that disappears beneath the waters of Cardigan Bay between Y Borth and Aberystwyth, owes its origin to the Dyfi glacier.

In Cardigan Bay a battle royal raged between opposing ice masses, for within its confines westerly-flowing ice streams from the Welsh mainland came into contact with a powerful ice-sheet bulldozing its way southwards along the floor of the Irish Sea basin. The Irish Sea ice-sheet, fed by glaciers emanating from the mountains of north-west and south-west Scotland, the Lake District and Northern Ireland, overran the entire coast south of Aberystwyth, leaving a visiting card in the form of boulder-clay cliffs, all containing far-travelled glacial erratics and shell fragments dredged off the floor of the Irish Sea, at centres such as Aber-arth, Aberaeron, New Quay (Ceinewydd), Mwnt and Gwbert. Following the opening in 2008 of the 96 kilometre-long Ceredigion Coast Path (Llwybr Arfordir Ceredigion), which winds its way up and over precipitous cliffs and across sandy bays between Cardigan and Ynys-las, those walkers and visitors prepared to sit and sort through beach pebbles washed out of the boulder-clay and associated sands and gravels will have their patience rewarded by the discovery amongst the blue-grey cobbles and pebbles of local sandstones and mudstones, of foreign stones: knobbly lumps of broken flints, gouged from layers of chalk outcropping on the floor of the Irish Sea; attractive igneous erratics from north-west Scotland; and rounded pebbles of Ailsa Craig microgranite, from the small island in the Firth of Clyde, once extensively quarried to make curling

1. Eryri as seen from the Cob; 2. Mochras, south-west of Llandanwg sand dunes

stones. The latter erratics are easily recognized by virtue of the fact that the light-grey, finely-crystalline igneous rock is bespeckled with darker blue-grey crystals of a mineral called riebeckite.

Because so much water was locked in ice caps and ice sheets that covered vast areas of northern Europe and North America, world-wide sea level at the height of the last 'ice age' was some 130 metres below its present level. As sea level fell at the onset not only of the last glaciation, but also earlier glacial episodes that punctuated the last two million years or so, the rivers draining into Cardigan Bay deepened their valley floors, a process later aided and intensified by the intense abrasive action of glaciers armed with huge quantities of broken and pulverized rock. Despite penetrating layer upon layer of glacial deposits and more recent sediments, a borehole sunk in the middle of the Mawddach estuary to a depth of 48 metres failed to encounter bedrock, whilst beneath the Teifi estuary the rock floor is at a depth in excess of 55 metres.

1. Lower reaches of Dyffryn Mawddach; 2. Cors Fochno; 3. Morfa Harlech and the mountains of Snowdonia

As the ice masses of the Devensian Glaciation began to melt and recede, sea level rose but not enough, at least initially, to prevent Bendigeidfran, 'king over the island of Britain', from walking across the Irish Sea basin on a desperate mission to rescue his sister Branwen, held captive by Matholwch, king of Ireland. The story is to be found in the Mabinogion, the collective name given to eleven medieval Welsh tales, four of which are known as 'The Four Branches of the Mabinogi'. During Bendigeidfran's reign, recalled during the second of the Four Branches, we are told that 'there were only two rivers, called the Lli and Archan' separating Wales from Ireland, but that 'later the sea spread out when it flooded the kingdoms'.

Although it's unlikely that the legend in the Mabinogion and the story of Cantre'r Gwaelod's fate preserves a folk memory of the post-glacial inundation of the territory between Wales and Ireland, both tales were doubtless an attempt by early inhabitants of the area to make sense of a strange and perplexing phenomenon. But for much later generations the submerged forest beds have proved to be a tangible and striking geological record of the time that sea level attained its present

level. And as the sea rose, so the rocks, washed out of the glacial deposits blanketing much of the floor of Cardigan Bay, were first swept landwards by the power of breaking waves. Then, following the stabilization of sea level about 6,000 years ago, the boulders, cobbles, pebbles and sand, have been carried northwards by wave action, driven by the prevailing south-westerly winds, to create a series of magnificent sandy beaches fronting shingle and sandy spits. The tongue of shingle that extends northwards between Y Borth and Ynys-las, is only prevented from reaching Aberdyfi's foreshore by the scouring action of the river Dyfi. Within the shelter of the spit lies Borth Bog (Cors Fochno), which in spite of peat extraction and agricultural reclamation in the past, remains the most extensive area of unmodified raised bog in Britain. Furthermore, its accumulated layers of organic and inorganic deposits are a repository of vital data recording climatic and environmental changes spanning the last 6,000 years.

Ro Wen, across the mouth of the Mawddach, is the counterpart of Y Borth spit. The sandy spit of Morfa Dyffryn, north of the seaside resort of Barmouth, attached its northern end to the boulder-clay island of Ynys Mochras as recently as 1830. North-east of the island stand the sombre grey walls of Harlech Castle. Built during the late thirteenth century by Edward I, the English king hell bent on subjugating the Welsh, the once formidable fortress has long since been left stranded atop a former rocky sea cliff by the growth of Morfa Harlech, a superb example of a sand spit developing across the Dwyryd–Glaslyn estuary. The sand, which has maintained the growth of the spit over the last 700 years, is probably derived from the thick pile of glacial deposits that floor the bay. The curving, c. six-kilometre sandy shore, backed by sand dunes, reclaimed coastal salt marshes and a line of old sea cliffs between Harlech and Talsarnau, is best viewed from Allt y Môr, a small cliff-top field owned by the National Trust and situated alongside the A496 at Llanfair, south-west of Harlech. It

1. *Mwnt: storm waves attacking the soft clay and gravel cliffs; 2. Fairbourne, a village destined to be lost to the sea;*
3. *Y Borth: Phase 1 of the coastal protection scheme was opened in March 2012 and Phase 2 in September 2015*

is one of the truly great vistas in Wales and on a clear day the panorama embraces the whole of the Llŷn peninsula as far as '*yr Wyddfa a'i chriw*' – Snowdon and its associated summits.

But such views are not immutable, for the sea continues to shape and reshape the coast. Furthermore, global warming and sea level rise are forecast to accelerate the scale and pace of coastal change. Reclaimed coastal lowlands, such as Morfa Harlech tucked in the north-east corner of Cardigan Bay and seaside villages such as Fairbourne (Y Friog), precariously located on the landward side of Y Friog spit, are particularly vulnerable to erosion in the face of a rising sea, currently predicted to be at least half a metre higher than its present level by the end of the twenty-first century. But no less vulnerable are cliffs fashioned from unconsolidated glacial deposits (the geological definition of a rock includes 'soft' materials such as clay, sand and gravel), such as those at Mwnt, a popular sandy beach at the southern end of Cardigan Bay.

Reputedly a pilgrimage church for those medieval pilgrims bound for Bardsey Island (Ynys Enlli), the supposed burial place of 20,000 saints at the tip of the Llŷn peninsula, the tiny, squat, whitewashed Church of the Holy Cross (Eglwys y Grog) at Mwnt is one of the oldest churches in Ceredigion. Built during the fourteenth century on a plug of boulder-clay and glacial sand and gravel infilling a pre-glacial valley, it nestles at the foot of Foel y Mwnt, a rocky hillock that rises 78 metres above sea level. A mere 80 metres or so west of the church, the plug of unstable glacial deposits, forming 25-metre-high cliffs at the back of the beach, is exposed to the full destructive fury of westerly gales. Cliff falls are a regular occurrence and with each fall, triggered by the relentless pounding action of waves, the cliff edges inexorably closer to the church.

Whilst little can be done to save the Church of the Holy Cross from the ravages of a rising sea, both the planned seaside town of Aberaeron – founded by Act of Parliament in 1807 and noted for its cheerfully-coloured terraces of late Georgian-style houses – and especially Y Borth have both been the subject of ambitious and costly coastal protection schemes. The construction of huge hard rock groynes, offshore reefs and masonry revetments have involved the transportation of enormous boulders from far and wide: dolerite from Minffordd, near Porthmadog, and the Clee Hills, near Ludlow (Llwydlo); sandstone from Ystradmeurig, north of Tregaron; limestone from Blaencilgoed, north of Amroth on the south Pembrokeshire coast, and over 40,000 tonnes of igneous rock armour from Norway. Worried locals and concerned visitors alike hope that the completed coastal defence works costing over £18 million in the case of Y Borth – costly and intrusive symbols of our profligate and unsustainable lifestyles – will ensure that both Aberaeron and Y Borth do not suffer, at least in the very near future, the same fate as the once fertile lands of Cantre'r Gwaelod that lie submerged beyond their shores.

Glossary

agglomerate a rock formed from the accumulation and consolidation of coarse volcanic material in the vicinity of a vent during an eruption

anticline an upfold similar in form to an arch

basalt a dark-coloured, fine-grained lava

bed a layer of sedimentary rock

columnar joints a pattern of parallel columns, polygonal in cross section, sometimes formed during the cooling and crystallization of basalt lava flows on the Earth's surface or sheets of dolerite that cooled within the Earth's crust

conglomerate a sedimentary rock mainly composed of rounded pebbles set in a matrix of sand

dolerite a dark-coloured, medium-grained igneous rock that has cooled and crystallized below the surface of the Earth

dome a fold in the form of a round, upturned saucer

fault a fracture where the rocks either side of the break have moved relative to one another

gabbro a dark-coloured, coarse-grained igneous rock that crystallized slowly deep within the Earth's crust

gneiss a metamorphic rock that is usually coarse-grained and is characterized by a layered appearance

granite a coarse-grained, light-coloured igneous rock that crystallized deep within the Earth's crust

igneous rock a rock formed as a result of the crystallization of magma (molten rock)

jasper a very finely crystalline variety of quartz, often red in colour

Last Glaciation the most recent major glacial period that was at its peak about 20,000 years ago

lava molten rock (magma) that has solidified on the Earth's surface

limestone a sedimentary rock composed mainly of calcium carbonate derived from the shells of animals that lived in shallow, clear, warm sea water

magma molten rock

metamorphic rock a rock, previously sedimentary or igneous, transformed by intense heat or pressure, or both

mudstone a sedimentary rock made of consolidated grains of mud

orogeny a period of mountain building

pillow lava heaped masses of lava resembling piles of pillows formed during a submarine volcanic eruption

quartz a very hard form of crystalline silica, often white in colour and occuring in veins in association with ore minerals

quartzite a hard sedimentary or metamorphic rock composed of quartz grains

rift valley an elongate lowland or valley tract bounded by faults

sandstone a sedimentary rock made of consolidated and cemented sand grains

schist a finely crystalline metamorphic rock that tends to split along parallel planes resulting from the parallel disposition of platy minerals

sedimentary rock rock formed by the consolidation of sediment, such as mud, sand and gravel, or the broken fragments of the shells of marine creatures in the case of organic limestone

shale a sedimentary rock composed of mud particles, that splits into thin layers

slate a fine-grained metamorphic rock that splits readily into thin sheets

subduction the movement of a dense, oceanic, tectonic plate under a less dense, continental, tectonic plate, so that the descending plate is consumed and destroyed

syncline a downfold similar in form to the cross section of a saucer

tuff/welded tuff a rock formed by the cooling and consolidation of dense clouds of red-hot volcanic dust and ash

Further reading

Bennett, Matthew, *Geology of Snowdonia*, The Crowood Press, 2007

Conway, John, *Rocks and landscapes of the Anglesey Coastal Footpath / Creigiau a thirluniau Llwybr Arfordirol Ynys Môn*, GeoMôn, 2010

Countryside Council for Wales, *Rocks / Creigiau*, Countryside Council for Wales, 2010

Downes, John, *Folds, Faults and Fossils: exploring geology in Pembrokeshire*, Llygad Gwalch, 2011

Elis-Gruffydd, Dyfed, *Wales: 100 Remarkable Vistas*, Y Lolfa, 2017

Gannon, Paul, *Rock Trails: Snowdonia*, Pesda Press Ltd, 2008

Gannon, Paul, *Rock Trails: South Wales*, Pesda Press Ltd, 2016

Howe, Stephen et al., *Walking the Rocks: Six walks discovering scenery & geology along the Glamorgan Coast*, Geologists' Association – South Wales Group, 2004

Lott, Graham and Barclay, Bill, *Geology and building stones in Wales (south) / Daeareg a cherrig adeiladu yng Nghymru (y de)*, British Geological Survey, 2002

Lott, Graham and Barclay, Bill, *Geology and building stones in Wales (north) / Daeareg a cherrig adeiladu yng Nghymru (y gogledd)*, British Geological Survey, 2002

Lynas, Bryan, *Snowdonia Rocky Rambles*, Sigma Leisure, 1996

Stevens, Terry, *Landscape Wales*, Graffeg, 2016

Thomas, Ian A. *Quarrying industry in Wales – a history / Y diwydiant Chwareli [sic] yng Nghymru – hanes*, The National Stone Centre, 2014

Thomas, Trevor M., *The Mineral Wealth of Wales and its Exploitation*, Oliver and Boyd Ltd, 1961

Toghill, Peter, *The Geology of Britain: an introduction*, Swan Hill Press, 2000

Treagus, Jack, *Anglesey Geology – a field guide / Daeareg Ynys Môn – arweinlyfr maes*, GeoMôn, 2008

Treagus, Jack E. and Treagus, Susan H., *The Rocks of Anglesey's Coast*, Gwasg Carreg Gwalch, 2013

Place names and Grid references

In Wales several places have Welsh and English names (Aberteifi, Cardigan; Caergybi, Holyhead) or Welsh names and English renditions (Caerffili, Caerphilly). Both appear on road-signs and over much of the country Welsh place-names rightly take precedence and appear above the English names. In the case where the Welsh and English names are significantly different to one another, the first use of the English name in each of the ten chapters is followed by the Welsh name in brackets. However, in the case of partially anglicized names, such as Solva (Solfa), Merthyr Tydfil (Merthyr Tudful) and Ewenny (Ewenni), only the Welsh names are included in the text.

For those readers unfamiliar with the geography of Wales, the following grid references will enable them, with the aid of the relevant 1:25,000 Ordnance Survey map, to locate each of the main places mentioned in the text:

1 Anglesey and the Llŷn peninsula
Aberdaron SH 173264
Amlwch SH 450933
Bardsey SH 116215
Gwalchmai SH 388762
Holyhead SH 248826
Llanddona SH 575795
Llanddwyn SH 387627
Llanfair-pwll SH 529771
Llanfair-yng-nghornwy SH 323909
Llangefni SH 460757
Llansadwrn SH 554759
Newborough SH 425656
Parys Mountain SH 445905
Porth Dinllaen SH 275415
Rhoscolyn SH 268757
South Stack SH 203823
Valley SH 292795

2 The St David's peninsula
Caerbwdi SM 766243
Caer-fai SM 761244
Carn Llidi SM 735279
Clegyr Boia SM 738252
Newgale SM 848223
Penbiri SM 767292
Pontypenyd SM 751257
Porth Clais SM 741241
Porth-gain SM 815325
Porth Lisgi SM 731237
Porth Mawr SM 733270
Porth Stinan SM 723252
Porth-y-rhaw SM 785242
St David's SM 753253
St David's Head SM 721279
Solfa SM 803243

3 The Harlech Dome and Snowdonia's 'Ring of Fire'
Aran Benllyn SH 867244
Aran Fawddwy SH 863224
Arennig Fawr SH 827370
Beddgelert SH 590481
Bethesda SH 625667
Bont-ddu SH 675189
Bwlch Tyddiad SH 659300
Capel Curig SH 725579
Carnedd Llywelyn SH 684644
Clogwyn Du'r Arddu SH 600555
Crib Goch SH 625553
Cwm Idwal SH 645598
Dolgellau SH 728177
Glyder Fawr SH 642580
Gwynfynydd SH 736284
Harlech SH 581312
Llanfair SH 576293
Moelwyn Mawr SH 658448
Nantlle 509533
Penygadair (Cadair Idris) SH 711130
Rhinog Fach SH 666270
Rhinog Fawr SH 656290
Rhobell Fawr SH 787257
Rhyd-ddu SH 569529
Snowdon SH 610544
Trawsfynydd SH 708356
Y Ganllwyd SH 727247

4 Rocks of the Welsh Basin: Cardigan Bay and the Elenydd Mountains
Aberystwyth SN 583817
Caban-coch SN 925645
Cardigan SN 179462
Cilgerran SN 195430
Cwmsymlog SN 705838
Cwmtydu SN 355576
Cwmystwyth SN 805748
Devil's Bridge SN 739770
Fron-goch SN 723745
Haverfordwest SM 955155
Llandovery SN 765345
Llangrannog SN 310542
Llanidloes SN 955845
Llanwrtyd SN 866474
Llechryd SN 218437
New Quay SN 390599
Penbryn SN 295519
Ponterwyd SN 748809
Pumlumon SN 790870
Rhayader SN 971680
St Dogmael's SN 165458
Tregaron SN 680597
Tre-saith SN 280515
Welshpool SJ 223076
Y Borth SN 609901
Y Fan SN 942877
Ystradmeurig SN 704676

5 Mynydd Hiraethog to the Dee estuary
Abergele SH 945775
Basingwerk Abbey SJ 196774
Betws-y-coed SH 795565
Brymbo SJ 295536
Caergwrle SJ 306575
Chirk SJ 290377
Denbigh SJ 055664
Dolgarrog SH 769676
Dyserth SJ 057789
Ffynnongroyw SJ 135823
Flint SJ 244730
Halcyn Mountain SJ 195716
Holywell SJ 185764
Llandegla SJ 195524
Llangollen SJ 215423
Moel Fama SJ 161626
Mwdwl Eithin SH 917540
Pentrefoelas SH 872515
Pontnewydd Cave SJ 015710
Prestatyn SJ 067827
Rhes-y-cae SJ 190709
Rhuddlan SJ 025782
Rhuthun SJ 124584
St Asaph SJ 036745
Talacre SJ 120844
Tremeirchion SJ 082730

6 Old Red Country: The Black Mountain and The Black Mountains
Brecon SO 045290
Cardiff ST 183768
Cribyn SO 025214
Cwmllynfell SN 748127
Cyfarthfa Castle SO 041073
Dôl-y-gaer SO 060145
Fan Fawr SN 970194
Fan Llia SN 939187
Fan Nedd SN 913184
Fan y Big SO 037207
Hay Bluff SO 244366
Llyn Cwm-llwch SN 001220
Llyn y Fan Fach SN 804219
Llyn y Fan Fawr SN 832215
Mynydd Illtud SN 962258
Neath SS 753977
Pen y Fan SO 012215

Pentwyn Reservoir SO 054150
Pontneddfechan SN 911081
Pont-sarn SO 045100
Pontsticill Reservoir SO 061120
Traeth Bach SN 965253
Traeth Mawr SN 968257
Trecastle SN 881291

7 The Valleys and the South Wales Coalfield
Aberdare SO 003026
Aber-fan SO 072000
Big Pit National Coal Museum SO 238087
Blaenafon SO 254090
Caerphilly ST 156871
Craig y Llyn SN 913037
Craig yr Hesg ST 075914
Cyfarthfa Castle SO 041073
Dowlais SO 065079
Ffos-y-frân SO 066063
Gilfach Goch SS 978895
Llyn Fawr SN 917035
Merthyr Tudful SO 050064
National Museum of Wales: Cardiff ST 183769
Neath SS 753977
Pontypridd ST 075900
St Bride's Bay SM 840163
Taff's Well ST 125833
Tonpentre SS 972954
Tower Colliery SN 927043

8 Rocks astride the Milford Haven Waterway
Abergavenny SO 298145
Caldey SS140963

Carew SN 047037
Carn Meini SN143326
Castlemartin SR 915984
Cobbler's Hole SM 805028
Cosheston SN 005037
Dale SM 812057
Freshwater East SS 020978
Freshwater West SR 883998
Grassholm SM 770072
Great Furzenip SR 887987
Kidwelly SN 407067
King's Quoit SS 059973
Lamphey SN 016005
Linney Head SR 883957
Little Furzenip SR 884993
Manorbier SS 065978
Marloes Sands SM 783074
Milford Haven SM 905059
Mill Bay SN 002050
Mynachlog-ddu SN144305
Norchard Beacon SN 073001
Old Castle Head SS 077966
Pembroke Dock SM 965035
Penally SS 118992
Priest's Nose SS 059972
Rosemarket SM 954085
St Ann's Head SM 807028
St Bride's Haven SM 802111
St Florence SN 083012
St Govan's Head SR 974926
Sandy Haven SM 860070
Skokholm SM 735050
Skrinkle Haven SS 080974
Tenby SN 132005
West Angle Bay SM 850033
West Dale Bay SM 798058

9 The Vale of Glamorgan
Barry Island ST 115665
Breaksea Point ST 023655
Bridgend SS 902800
Caerphilly ST 156871
Cardiff ST 183768
Cwm Bach SS 898718
Cwm Nash SS 907702
Dunraven SS 884731
Ewenni SS 912778
Flemingston ST 016701
Kidwelly SN 407067
Lavernock Point ST 189679
Llancarfan ST 051702
Llandaff Cathedral ST 155781
Llantwit Major SS 968688
National Museum of Wales: Cardiff ST 183769
Nash Point SS 914683
Neath Abbey SS 737973
Ogmore-by-sea SS 865750
Ogmore Castle SS 882770
Penarth ST 185715
St Dogmael's Abbey SN 164458
St Mary's Well Bay ST 180677
Swanbridge ST 169673
Swansea Castle SS 657931
Tresilian Bay SS 947677
Trwyn y Witsh SS 884726

10 Cardigan Bay and Cantre'r Gwaelod
Aberaeron SN 458628
Aber-arth SN 479638
Aberdyfi SN 615960
Aber-mawr SM 880347
Aberystwyth SN 583817

Arennig Fawr SH 827370
Bardsey SH 116215
Barmouth SH 612158
Blaencilgoed SN 155106
Borth Bog SN 630910
Cardigan Bay SN 540900
Clarach SN 587838
Dolgellau SH 728177
Fairbourne SH 618128
Fishguard SM 956371
Gwbert SN 161498
Harlech SH 581312
Hengwrt SH 723188

Llanfair SH 576293
Llwyngwril SH 591097
Minffordd SH 596385
Morfa Dyffryn SH 560245
Morfa Harlech SH 575335
Mwnt SN 194519
Newgale Sands SM 847220
Newport Bay SN 030410
New Quay SN 389598
Porthmadog SH 567386
Ro Wen SH 610135
Talsarnau SH 612359
Tonfannau SH 561036

Traeth Mawr SH 585395
Tremadog Bay SH 540340
St David's Point SM 721278
Sarn Badrig SH 550261
Sarn Gynfelyn SN 590857
Sarn y Bwch SH 560035
Y Borth SN 608898
Ynys-las SN 607928
Ynys Mochras SH 554265
Ystradmeurig SN 704676

Acknowledgements

The author wishes to thank not only Myrddin ap Dafydd, of Gwasg Carreg Gwalch, for asking me to undertake the writing of this book but also to those listed below who have kindly provided some of the many illustrations.

Peter Appleton of the Brymbo Heritage Group; Bryony Chambers-Towers, British Geological Survey; Alison Davies, Mapping Company Ltd.; David Evans, photographer, for the images of Craig y Delyn and Sarn Gynfelyn; Rhian Kendall, British Geological Survey; Raymond Roberts, Natural Resources Wales; Georgina Taubman, Liason Officer, Miller Argent (South Wales).

My thanks too to those few good friends, including my wife Siân, who have been a constant source of encouragement.

Unless otherwise stated, the photographs are the property of Dyfed Elis-Gruffydd and Siân Bowen.